Dark Psychology Secret

Everyday Practical Guide on How to Analyze
People and Stop being Manipulated with
Emotional Deception, Mind Control, NLP
Techniques, Brainwashing, Mind Games

Anastasia Kinsky

Brian J. Fox

Dark Psychology Secrets

To my father, Giuseppe,
who inspired to imagine and create.

Dark Psychology Secrets

TABLE OF CONTENTS

Dark Psychology Secrets

"Knowing your own darkness is the best method for dealing with the darknesses of other people."

– C. G. Jung

Introduction

Congratulations on purchasing this book, Dark Psychology Secret, and thank you for picking out this book.

Do you want to learn how not to be controlled and dominated by manipulating, lying, selfish, and unreliable people? Do you wish to develop your ability to recognize and avoid them? Do you know people who have huge egos and only think about their needs? Do you want to drive out those that tyrannize and scare others (this only embodies their weakness and inability to have a healthy relationship)? If you know someone like this in your life, such as an office colleague or your boss at work, your partner or a friend, and a parent or another family member, this book will be helpful to solve your problems.

Dark Psychology Secret offers you valuable tips that are easy to implement and essential tools to use with any of these types of people. This book is an essential guide for learning how to detect all the characteristics and behavior models that these horrible people use. This book will help you to unmask the true motivations that lie behind the deceptive façade of psychopaths. It will help you to effectively get rid of the victim's role through a wide range of methods and discover why these people have become a part of our lives. This book proposes a way to escape them forever.

When you hear the word 'manipulation,' you may think something like: "Wait, isn't this wrong?"

It isn't since manipulation is just a tool some people use to their advantage. How you utilize this tool can identify whether it's right or wrong. For instance, an example of manipulation being inappropriate is doing something that gets somebody injured. There are some unwritten rules that you should not break when it comes to manipulation. Specialists work to understand better why and how evil people work and to what end. They also try to learn why we idolize these psychopaths. It is essential to be aware that every one of us has a "Dark" or "Light" side.

If you maintain an ethical approach, then

manipulation can end up being a technique of better understanding these individuals, while also knowing how to collaborate with them instead of them using you. You can even use it for useful reasons, such as influencing or convincing other people. An example of someone that did this was Steve Jobs, who used his influencing ways to get what he wanted done. He would undoubtedly convince his employees that it was possible to do something that people thought almost impossible. Because of his influencing skills, this would make them work harder towards his end goal, and eventually bring about a brand-new mark in the technology field.

Here we will explore the more sordid and dark aspects of the human psyche, as well as some methods of applying our knowledge for use in our everyday lives. We will explore the following areas that are principles of "Dark psychology": Dark personality traits, studies of dark psychology, Art of Persuasion and Manipulation in history, and Dark Triad and Psychopathy in our daily lives (Family, Work, Friends, and Online).

The ability to control individuals is a valuable skill to master. It is just one of the reasons how businesspeople, as well as political leaders, get and maintain their present positions. There comes a time in your life where you need to turn off your feelings as well as be pragmatic. These skills are abilities you should learn and practice. It's not easy to discuss this because we, as a society, have this fear of the truth; that people can get used as a means to an end.

The techniques used in Dark Psychology are some of the most effective forces at work. Not only in this era but even in the past. Ethically, as well as socially problematic behavior, becomes part of day-to-day life. Callous, selfish, unscrupulous, or even downright wicked behavior, can easily be found across history, as well as throughout various cultures. We didn't invent anything special or unique to just us. From the ancient Chinese wisdom in the "Art of War," to Greeks and Romans, as well as Freud and Jung, the most important and successful influencers have always used these techniques. Those who don't see the benefits of using this end up getting it used against them. So, it's an urge for those that don't try this end up risking.

If you decide to lift the curtain on dark psychology, you can never go back to the way things were. We must be spectators and actors of the drama to understand human beings that very few people ever gain.

People that use "dark tactics" regularly manipulate and influence us to get their desired outcomes. Are you ready to use it in your life? Dark Psychology Secret talks not only about art but also about the science of manipulation and mind control. Psychology discusses mainly the human behavior that is a study of our thoughts, actions, and interactions with other people. Dark Psychology is the way that these people use tactics of persuasion, manipulation, motivation, and coercion to get what they desire. What do you think makes manipulation so effective? Can mind control and brainwashing help us? You can get all these answers by reading this book.

Thank you again for choosing Dark Psychology Secrets. We hope you will enjoy it. We would like to hear your thoughts with a short review on Amazon.

We have a lot of ground to cover, so we should now dive into our first subject regarding dark psychology: its principles.

"My friends, it is wise to nourish the soul; otherwise, you will breed dragons and devils in your heart."

– C. G. Jung

Chapter 1: What is Dark Psychology?

When we think about "Dark Psychology," our thoughts generally fly to the most aggressive, or lustful, anti-social instincts: rape, murder, incest, treason, sadism, masochism, etc. However, your darkest fantasies may not be all that daemonic.

It is time we looked at our so-called "Dark Side" from a whole new perspective.

Psychology is an understanding of how the human mind works, and it is a part of all of our lives. It includes everything in our lives from love and hate, finance and advertising, and even crime and religion.

Dealing with this is not an easy task sometimes because we are not so brave to see over the curtain.

Why do you think is it so important to know what Dark Psychology is? Most of you will answer that it is necessary because someone may use that power and knowledge against you. This could be a good reason!

Maybe you have chosen this book because you want to learn how to work with people from the inside out. You would like to know how to say just the right thing at the right moment. This book will help you get what you need and show you how to manipulate people such that you can overpass any obstacles, so they will do what you want. There is no judgment on the reason why you want to read and learn from this book. Anyway, you came to the right place.

Dark psychology is any deviant or criminal behavior that is committed against others, usually innocent victims. The one who is going to use Dark Psychology will prey on someone who they see as weak or vulnerable. It doesn't mean they are weak, but the benefits are that the manipulator can easily influence them.

Being able to understand dark psychology is not just a defensive measure. There are a lot of principles and techniques in the world of dark psychology.

Steve Jobs was very well known for his ability to work with people's emotions. He used to say just the right thing at the right moment that would get them to come around to his view. He was so effective that the people used to say: the 'reality distortion field,' a phrase used from the first time in the Star Trek universe.

We have a myriad of historical instances of Steve Jobs taking advantage of his fantastic ability to get what he wanted. In the 1980s, Steve Jobs was trying to get Pepsi CEO John Sculley to come to Apple. Jobs said: "Do you want to sell sugared water for the rest of your life, or do you want to come with me and change the world?"

He had a unique talent to manipulate and charm people, adding to a deep comprehension of what people wanted and what people wanted to hear. If you combine the knowledge of power management, subtle intimidation, and a large amount of charisma and passion, and you have a magnet that could attract pretty much whatever he wanted.

In this book, we will analyze the most sordid part of our mind, mentioning some of the major fathers of the theory of the "Dark Side" and cases related to our daily life. Sometimes in a cruel way and sometimes in a humorous way with exhilarating examples, to make the subject relevant but not so heavy, as it seems to be.

The main purpose of this book is to allow us to learn more about ourselves, about our inner parts and, to analyze the behavior of the people close to us. Only understanding or trying to reveal some of our hidden parts can we start to be aware of the world around us.

"Jokingly, we can say everything, even the truth."

— *Sigmund Freud*

In the book Civilization and Its Discontents (1929), Sigmund Freud stated that being a part of civilized society protects us from personal chaos, from being subdued by our amoral desire. Sigmund Freud was psychoanalysis's father. He applied a clinical method for treating psychopathology with dialogue between a patient and psychoanalysis.

We designate public authorities (e.g., police) to protect us not merely from others' impulses but even from our own. Freud thinks that it is a necessary protection that creates our "malcontent," which then requires us to dominate our compass for the pleasure-seeking instinctual. Living harmoniously

in our society, we have to control our impetuous wishes.

"Most people do not really want freedom, because freedom involves responsibility, and most people are frightened of responsibility."

— *Sigmund Freud*

Although it could look somewhat trivialized, we can find something good in Freud's ideas about our minds. Meanwhile, I think that we may be made to at least conceive how it will be to follow our inborn desires, regardless of how we might affect others. Just imagining ourselves in such behaviors doesn't mean that we will apply it.

Anyway, we need to confide in others to survive. We're a human species, and we feel the need to be "good," so we don't do things that might offend others and turn away them. Although we cannot stop our imagination about a gesture that might permit us to follow our "innate pleasure," most of us have a strong motivation to repress ourselves to enact this sociopathic behavior.

Given these "natural" internal limitations, we should ask whether our dark side is, ultimately, all that dark. That is, we're generally aware that independently from the image we may have of power, conquest, revenge, or reckless expression of libido are just that—imagination or fantasies. Allowing ourselves only to dream about it, we can permit ourselves some alternative gratuity. In safe mode, removing these acts from our daily life, we can give ourselves the alternative image of what, in reality, we wouldn't choose to do, or, to be.

"The virtuous man contents himself with dreaming that which the wicked man does in actual life."

— *Sigmund Freud*

In this way, we can consider our dark side; let's say, "innocent." Allowing it to resurface in our daydreams, offers us a way to escape from a social behavior that almost all of us regularly choose to take part in — all this effort to maintain our social status in a strongbox. And even if we may have a competitive vein in us, we also give high value on interpersonal collaboration. Voluntarily, we control our impulses to keep them monitored.

We periodically allow ourselves to create a world in which our desire—however extravagant or anti-social—might yet live.

Our dark side grows in our more primitive, pleasure or power-seeking instincts, must we ardently avoid rejecting it as degraded—something other than human worthy and therefore to be banned and denied? In the end, such a "dark" desire can't be as inherently guilty; usually, it represents an innate "appetite" or "impetus" in all of us.

In the end, should we honor them, appreciating our most aggressive or erotic fantasies, daydreams or night dreams, as a psychological safety valve? For me, the unsatisfactory alternative is to judge them deplorably, as showing a part of us so dark that it has to be unseen from others—and, maybe, even from our knowledge.

Many psychologists wrote about the fundamental utility of daydreams. For, as already suggested, they can work positively as a much-needed release from our frustrations. Giving us at least a hidden impression of impulses and inclinations that we know would be dangerous to act out. Our mere fantasies don't reflect any potential catastrophe recognized as dark or depraved.

"Everyone carries a shadow, and the less it is embodied in the individual's conscious life, the blacker and denser it is."

– *Carl G. Jung*

Because of this hidden desire, it is why horror movies are always popular, especially among the younger population. Even the film can allow us to experience a safe liberation from our more primitive and anti-social instincts. This is the truth for many movies or tv series (e.g., "Hannibal" and "Dexter").

We are, in the end, all animals. What allows us to surpass our primitive, less evolved ancestors is our developed interest in social behavior. Most of us freely agreed to renounce this kind of pleasure because we realize that it could hurt others and ourselves.

For our inner and outer balance, we have a fundamental need to express our whole being. And we hardly need to deny our "forbidden" thoughts. They're only a relatively small segment of what is—naturally—inside us. Fully accepting the basic human needs that we have recognized and making peace with it becomes our "dark side." We can now consider it less dark when we understand it for what it is.

It makes perfect sense that if creativity involves absolute freedom from our common bond in thought and feeling, then giving ourselves the approval to create and the privilege to inner thoughts can show us the darker side of our hidden tendencies and impulses.

Maybe what makes a work of art great is the globality of the message. And the reason for the universality is that it talks deeply with what resides in us: the sinful and unnamable, as well as the praiseworthy, noble, and wholesome.

"In spite of its function as a reservoir for human darkness—or perhaps because of this—the shadow is the seat of creativity."

– Carl G. Jung

Notes:

_____
_____
_____
_____
_____
_____
_____
_____
_____
_____
_____
_____
_____
_____
_____
_____
_____
_____
_____
_____
_____
_____
_____
_____
_____
_____
_____

"I think the healthy way to live is to make friends with the beast inside oneself, and that means not the beast but the shadow. The dark side of one's nature. Have fun with it, and you know, is to accept everything about ourselves."

— *Anthony Hopkins*

Chapter 2: Investigating personalities

When first understanding how others might persuade us and how we might be able to influence them, we should figure out what makes up different personality types. There are the people who can become easily manipulated and the people who do the manipulating, or so it seems. A person can be both, and it is up to you to find a way to be aware of your behavior to make sure that you are in charge of your actions and emotions.

Some manipulators don't even realize what they are doing. Others are skilled, living in a delusional world where everyone is like a stringed puppet, and they are the master. If you want to make sure that you can become free of this kind of control, then it is essential to understand the personalities that are making up these kinds of interactions.

A lot of manipulative individuals have similar qualities, no matter how different they might look amongst each other. It is often hard to tell because their behavior is so secretive. They know how to control things behind the scenes, to their advantage.

Many manipulative individuals love the fact that they can discuss your good and bad qualities with others behind your back. The defining characteristic of such manipulators is that they tend to put everything about you in a bad light when talking about you with others. If someone is often gossiping about others around you, then you can be assured that they are going to be gossiping about you just the same. In some instances, they might even be playing both sides, using both of you on either end of the gossip as a piece in their entertaining game. They will regularly discuss you with others, even if it seems as though the two of you have some confidence when they converse with you about others.

They don't understand the idea of limits. For them, there is no limit to what they can achieve. They will stop at nothing to get the things that they desire, no matter who they might end up hurting along the way.

The only thing that some manipulators are interested in is filling their wants so they can feel powerful. They will ignore your limits and push you past the point at which you feel comfortable. No matter how resistant you might be, they will still push you further. They are interested in seeing just how far they can take things, which means they will stop at nothing to fulfill their curiosities.

Manipulators don't like to listen to what they are doing or to discover that someone understood their plans. They are the ones who would like to be in complete control. Even when authority figures aren't directly reaching out to them and trying to tell them what to do, they can still feel very threatened with their power. They can take the slightest remark as someone trying to attack their character, and they will never stop to make sure that they feel powerful. They have no care for whoever they have to hurt. Even a slight suggestion could be triggering and end up setting them off.

They will pretend to understand you, but never really will. Some are skilled actors who might trick you into thinking they are passionate human beings. In reality, this can be their attempt to have you falling even more under their control. They will make you feel as though they want to connect to you, only so they can become closer and have a stronger grip.

Manipulative individuals will want the things that they can't have, so sometimes that means pretending to be someone else. Some individuals will put on different faces for the right setting. Others will know how to manipulate the setting so that it aligns with their current personality.

They will pretend to listen to you, try and relate, and practice showing empathy, but deep down, that is not who they are. A manipulator will end up still being manipulative and controlling, using even some of the information shared with you against you at one point. These individuals can be narcissists, psychopaths, and other deeply manipulative people who wish to take power from you and keep it for themselves.

Manipulative conduct includes three variables: dread, commitment, and blame. When somebody is manipulating you, you are in effect mentally pressured into accomplishing something you presumably would prefer not to do. You may feel frightened to do it, commit to doing it, or blameworthy about not doing it.

When it comes to controlling individuals, some are good at harassing you, while others might end up making themselves the victim in the end. Someone who is rather controlling will make you feel scared, using hatred, threats, and other terrors as a means to control you. While they do this, they can even end up making you feel the blame.

In other cases, the controller might be the one who tries to be the victim. They might act hurt by what you said, heightening their emotions to make you look like the bad guy. In reality, they are usually the ones that caused the issue in the first place. By controlling the situation, to suit their needs, they become the person in charge, quickly manipulating the situation to best suit their own needs.

Common Manipulators

Following are some personality qualities of manipulative individuals, so you'll realize what to look for when one comes your way. Understanding these fundamental traits can help keep you from getting tricked into a manipulative relationship.

Remaining cautious, keeping in contact with what you know to be the reality about yourself, and understanding your worth can help to empower you to stay away from these individuals.

Some of the most common types of manipulators include narcissists, psychopaths, and sociopaths. The main difference between the three is how they choose to share their feelings and the image that they will put up to protect who they are.

Narcissists are probably the most common of these types of people. They will not have any concern for others and instead only care about protecting themselves and their identities. Rather than listening and caring about who you are and what it is that you might have to say, they will instead only be concerned about their feelings, doing their best to ensure their needs are satisfied.

A psychopath works a little harder. They will ensure that you are under their complete control, and they have a way of making you feel terrible about yourself all while they have a smile on their faces.

These types of individuals will rarely show their true colors and will instead put up a fake image of who they are. They won't show when they are angry and will do their best to protect their image, even if it means acting irrationally or in a foul way.

A sociopath is the one who is least concerned with their image. They will actively freak out in front of others, and they will never care how their angry outbursts might end up affecting other people.

These are standard manipulators' behaviors, and they all have similar qualities. They will only focus on the things that matter to them, and they have little disregard for you. It is relevant to note that these people don't care less about others because they don't like those individuals. A narcissist won't ignore your needs because they despise you. They lack the skills needed to understand what a person is going through.

They are persevering in the quest for what they need and have little respect for who gets injured along the way. Jamming into your space— physically, inwardly, mentally, or profoundly is of no worry to them.

You can compare them to a parasite. In our world, this is regularly an adequate relationship.

But benefiting from somebody due to that person's detriment is draining, debilitating, devastating, and disparaging.

It isn't so much that manipulative individuals don't understand what their responsibility is in any given relationship. They do; a manipulative individual observes nothing wrong with shirking liability for their actions, even while making you assume accountability for yours.

For this reason, they are often presenting double standards that can be draining, confusing, and exhausting. What is OK behavior for them is unacceptable for you, and vice versa. It is almost impossible to reason with these types of individuals.

Highly Sensitive People

Manipulative individuals go after our sensibilities, passions, and principles. They will readily pick out your weaknesses. They will see if you have something that might upset you, a topic you like to avoid, or a specific area that makes you uncomfortable.

They can exploit this weakness to tap into your vulnerability and find a way to use that to their advantage. They will then attack your passions. They will see that you are an empathetic and caring person, and on both a conscious and subconscious level, they will exploit that, as well. Finally, they will attack your character, virtue, and other standards that make up your life, so you no longer have a unique identity and instead serve their ideologies.

All feelings, regardless of whether positive or negative, fill a need in our voyages. We need to be aware of individuals who utilise the compelling intensity of emotions to manipulate you. If you recognize as an empath, this will mainly apply to you, as this type of individual is most defenseless against negativity from others. Next time you feel badly misused, use the tips we have throughout this book for protecting yourself.

A highly sensitive person can more easily feel the emotions of others and might feel more upset when sensing that others are feeling negative. An empath can have the same sense, yet this term is useful in a somewhat metaphysical sense, and they can relate to a psychic.

Individuals who enjoy toying with others' feelings will utilize any strategies, perplexities, faults, and cross-examinations, for example, to indeed make you feel uncomfortable.

They realize that they have a decent possibility of guiding you into a relationship since you are a thoughtful individual who likes to help others. They may take into account your integrity and consideration at first, frequently praising you for the great individual you are.

However, after some time, recognition of these characteristics will be limited since you are they are using you, and they don't care about you. They only care about what you can accomplish for them.

Highly sensitive people, or those who can sometimes be referred to simply as empaths, are the ones who struggle the most against manipulators. It is almost as if manipulators see that empaths have so much compassion to give that they are attempting to heal their inner demons with it; only they go about it in the worst possible way.

If you need to manage these sorts of individuals regularly, like in your working environment, overlook them or astonish them by saying something pleasant as opposed to meeting them with a confrontational frame of mind. Compulsive controllers flourish off aggravating you, so ensure you don't give them what they need—after a few fizzled endeavours, they may start to disregard you.

Positive Manipulative Personalities

Not all manipulation is inherently destructive or toxic. It is necessary to learn the differences between manipulation, persuasion and influencing. While this chapter may be intense, it is a warning against the dangers of manipulation and what can happen when others are not as cautious with how they are using this vital tool.

Throughout the rest of the book, we are going to teach you to recognize manipulation as we know it now. It can become more malicious and dangerous and can end up taking over the lives of other people. When not used properly, it can damage relationships and put a strain on many individual lives. It can be used for ruthless purposes and to get selfish desires fulfilled.

When you use manipulation for the benefit of others, it may be in the form of influence and persuasion. It begins with persuasion. You can encourage others to do good things by showing the different benefits of the outcome that you are guiding them to. Sometimes, persuasion needs to be used even on ourselves, as it can be challenging to start to do the things that we know are best for ourselves.

Once a person gains a high level of

persuasiveness, they can become an influencer. These are the people who can help shape the world, change lives, and keep people mindful of a more positive and healthy perspective. When manipulation can be recognized, understood, and turned to a more positive light, it can make for a happy life and a much better world.

Negative manipulation is easy. Our brains can sometimes even do it without us noticing. If someone tells you good news, but you react poorly because the good news might harm you, then that can be very subtle manipulation against the other person. For example, a mother hearing that her child got accepted to a university, several states away might react poorly because of her own emotion about missing her child. It's still good news, and the mother may know that rationally. But the child then sees that mom isn't happy with this decision and will choose to not go to this school because of mom's negative, emotional response.

The mother might not have intended to react that way and only did based on emotion, but it was still something that negatively influenced her daughter. A more positive impact on that situation would take place if the mother told her daughter how happy she was for her, and then had a more severe discussion later of the challenges that living several states away from your mother can present to a first-year college student. In this situation, it allows the daughter to make still her own decision outside of what others want. She might even choose to stay home, but if she does, that is an important decision she made for herself without being manipulated.

The better we can understand what manipulation is and how we can use it for ourselves, it will become easier to have a life in harmony with others. You will be able to better understand for yourself the things that you want, and you will know how to get those results better. Rather than pushing people away or straining relationships because of the difficulty in getting what you want, you can pull people closer and have them depend on you for positive and healthy influence.

"When a person cannot deceive himself the chances are against his being able to deceive other people"

– Mark Twain

Notes:

_____
_____
_____
_____
_____
_____
_____
_____
_____
_____
_____
_____
_____
_____
_____
_____
_____
_____
_____
_____
_____
_____
_____
_____
_____
_____
_____
_____
_____
_____

"Everybody has the ability to be manipulative, to be hateful and deceitful. "

— *Neil LaBute*

Chapter 3: Manipulation

Manipulation is the art to influence or control people cleverly or unscrupulously. We have all manipulated someone or a situation for a desirable outcome. It sounds quite dark but let me tell you a story from my infancy.

I had a way of opportunely falling sick when I didn't want to go to school. In the beginning, my parents immediately took action, and they cared about me. After three emergency trips to the clinic, my mother suspected my antics. The next few times, she brought me to the hospital, but she didn't allow me to stay home anymore. In one of my fake cases, my friends told me that my favorite football player got invited to the school for a visit. I pray my mother to be taken back to school, forgetting that I had "an unbearable tummy ache." My mom didn't give me any chances to go to school and advised me to remain at home. Nothing could change her mind, not even after I admitted to faking my stomach pains. When I got to school the day after, I was green with envy when my friends showed me all the cool things that they received. Suffice it to say that I never faked sickness again to escape going to school.

This example from school is just one of many cases I can write about things that we do to manipulate people and situations. I know many adults who still fake the flu to get a day off work.

Manipulation is not entirely wrong, especially when you manipulate someone to get a good result for them.

The art of manipulation is in our nature, but when it comes to psychological manipulation, things get darker and more sinister. A person's actions or thoughts are influenced by the use of underhanded tactics that are either abusive, deceptive, or even both. The manipulated person isn't given a choice to either accept or reject the will of the manipulator.

Manipulators have their reasons for acting how they do. It could be for getting financial gains like the fake policeman who decided to take my neighbor's money. In their workplace, these people are busy to further their agendas, even if it would mean ruining other people's lives.

Their principle is elementary; get what you want; it doesn't matter if you farm other people.

In personal relationships, it is usually about getting power and staying in control. And last but not least, someone manipulates others for a recreative aim. They use their games to pass the time and prevent boredom. It is crude and vicious, but this mentality reflects their thought processes.

Lying is one of the most effective tools used by them. A good manipulator is skilled in the art of deception. He or she is adept at coming up with grand stories that have no real bearings on the truth. Or one goes for deceit and lies omitting some information. Some manipulators are so good at their lies that you rarely realize the lie until it is too late. Another tactic employed by manipulators is shaming and guilt-tripping.

When uncovered for something they have done wrong, they instantly refuse it and then turn the tables around by making you promptly feel bad for asking them. They vilify their prey and to further strengthen their hold on their victim; they can turn the victim into the abuser effectively. Unfortunately, we would find this kind of manipulative technique in domestic lives where the abuser blames the victim's character, words, or actions that were prompted by his or her behavior in the first place.

Other subtle techniques used in manipulation include the use of, non-committal and evasive answer to asked questions. It is also common that they will act rationally, and when they get caught, they will revolve the reality to match their narrative. Some manipulators use sex and seduction to obtain their devious objectives. When caught with the hands in the proverbial cookie jar, projection and anger of blame are quickly used to reverse the case for their advantage.

However, manipulators are often not casual in their selection of the victim. There are precise traits in their prey that attract them, and particular weaknesses also make it easier for manipulators to perpetuate their hunting. Lonely people with weak self-esteem and an eagerness to please are easier to control than the assertive social type. For such people, manipulators study their personality and weaknesses before using it against them. This facade easily fools emotional people. Arrogant people who make compulsive solutions are easier to be manipulated, taking actions that have long term impact. People who are avid and materialistic have a higher tendency of being cheated.

Deception

Deception is the art of concealing the truth, to gain benefits. It can look like manipulation, but, there is a defined difference. It is often used in manipulation and is one of the many layers in a manipulator's checklist. Deception aims to trick and fool the prey.

A lier may take a long time before it is detected, but when it is, the harm and damages can be disastrous.

I know a story of a man who had been married for over 30 years. From the marriage, they had three children between the ages of 12 and 17. Everything was rosy for the family. The kids went to the best schools and enjoyed a luxuries life thanks to the wealth obtained through years of hard work and resilience by this man. He grew his children by ensuring that whatever they needed, even spoiling them. And who could blame him? For the first six years, the couple was unable to have a baby. They asked the help of consultants, priests, and even tried some different procedure all to no avail. At a certain point, when the marriage was at an all-time low, his wife got pregnant. He was overjoyed. When the couple had two more children, it felt as though life could not get any better, but it happened.

His wealth grew exponentially, and everything was perfect. One day, the family got a call that their eldest son had an accident. A lifesaving operation that involved organ transplantation was necessary to survive. When the man was donating his organ to save his child, he discovered the terrible secret his wife had kept for many years. The child was not his. None of the children were his. Hurt, broken, and ashamed, he took his own life, but not without cutting off his wife and children from his wealth. This deception started as a lie to one person, but at the end of the day, five people (including the deceiver) were affected by it. Besides, the pain experienced by the extended family, friends, and colleagues also impacted others.

In a different case, a new startup firm employed an accountant to manage their finances. The owner of the startup gradually increases his trust in the young accountant. It was a combination of a strictly business relationship and a sense of friendship. As the company grew and expanded its activity, the business owner entrusted most of the administrative responsibilities to the accountant. He proved competent and was committed to even more responsibilities. These responsibilities came with many perks and benefits. For years life was going well. One day a failed transaction drove a quick check on the company's records; the owner was unprepared for the surprise that uncovered. He and his company, over the years, had been systematically ransacked, reducing the company's accounts in the red. The young accountant ran away, and he was left to clean up the mess. Within months, the company folded up. Forty-three people lost their jobs, the business owner lost all of his investment, and relinquished his ability to trust.

The crude fact is that deception builds upon the very emotion that is essential for human relationships: trust between the deceiver and the victim. The higher the confidence, the greater the betrayal. And when there is a deep betrayal, the destructive impact often goes beyond the two individuals involved.

However, deception isn't always something that happens to others. Sometimes, it encompasses the lies we tell ourselves. We justify specific actions with the deep lies we tell. Just like manipulation, lying is also something that everyone does. Some of us may have developed certain moral principles that make it difficult for us to tell blatant lies or associate with people who do so. But it doesn't stop us from telling lies, albeit "little" lies. Knowing the answer to a question but choosing to deny knowledge of it in a bid to preserve one's social grace is a lie.

Let me explain: let's say you witnessed your boss toss your colleague's project [something that he or she worked hard for] in the trash and you listened as the colleague talked extensively about how horrible he or she thought the idea was. You hum and ham and then you leave the office only to be confronted by the colleague who enquires about the boss's thoughts on the project. Telling the truth in this example would do more harm than good. And so, you lie. Your intention to deceive your colleague was for his or her protection.

In dark psychology, the intent to deceive presents more benefits to the deceiver than it does to the victim. As mentioned earlier, manipulators use deception to strengthen their hold on their victims. For deceivers, the deception gives them an opening into developing a relationship with the victim. The goal is to exploit this relationship for their benefits. One of the most recent forms of deception employed today is deceptive affection — people claiming to feel more love or emotion for you than they do.

There are not many things that one can use to describe the feeling of being told that someone loves you. The feeling of love is especially gratifying for people who have craved this experience. The liar gets the benefits of declaring this false affection in the form of trust, sex, and sometimes money.

Hypnosis

Once upon a time, the idea of hypnosis was relegated to the world of make-believe that the swinging of an object could control a person's mind, and the snapping of fingers was considered a disbelieving idea. My first encounter with hypnosis was at a magic show. The magician called a member of the audience on stage, and then he put "her under." In that state, she did some weird things that I am pretty sure she would have been too mortified to do in her right senses. When he snapped her out of it, she had no idea what had transpired in the last 2 minutes. To acknowledge that someone could have that much power over you and cause you to do things you ordinarily would not do is frightful. So, I understand why we have chosen to deny it.

However, no amount of denial can change the fact that hypnosis is real and used much more frequently than we care to admit. In today's modern psychology, hypnotherapy has been effective in the treatment of certain skin conditions and during the management of pain associated with childbirth, dental procedures, and even rheumatoid arthritis. While hypnosis is undoubtedly not your average "pat on the cheek and do as I say" type of move, certain people are more susceptible to hypnosis than others. But let's not get ahead of ourselves.

Hypnosis in psychology is a cooperative interaction in which the participants respond to the suggestions of the hypnotist. That is to say, when a person becomes hypnotized, the hypnotist deeply guides his or her actions. In the movies, we are made to believe that a person under hypnosis becomes sleepy and disoriented. In reality, people react differently under hypnosis, but they are not as incapacitated as they appear. Psychologists define it as a state of hyper-awareness. In this state, they experience focused attention, heightened suggestibility, and vivid fantasies. People end up in this state with the use of visualization and verbal repetition.

Hypnosis tells us that not everyone is easily hypnotized [clearly, you need to possess a keen ability to visualize things]. A recent study estimates the percentage of people [adults] who cannot get hypnotized at 10%. That leaves about 90% of us susceptible, which is shocking considering how strongly a lot of us feel about hypnotism. I suspect that some of the negative feelings we have about hypnotism are due to wrongly held beliefs about it. Here are some of the common misjudgments we have:

1. Hypnotism puts you under the complete control of your hypnotist.

In the movies, we are made to believe a person who is down under would have his or her actions controlled by the hypnotist. In reality, this is not true. While hypnosis relies heavily on suggestions, if your mind is not in agreement with those suggestions, you would generally reject it outright. So, no. You will not be crawling on all fours and mooing like a cow...not unless you want to do so.

2. Someone may not be able to snap out of hypnosis.

The mind is more complicated than we make it out to be. The same self-protective mechanisms that render it almost impossible for your hypnotist to control your actions also keep you alert, and if there is any immediate danger, you can snap out of it in a moment's notice.

3. Hypnosis is some dark magic or spiritual event.

Sorry to disappoint you, but this is merely science. Hypnosis comes from research by the work of renowned psychologists like Sigmund Freud. There are methods and processes to it, and none of it requires wooden dolls and red candles. All that is needed is your consent.

4. You can become hypnotized against your will.

Again, we have Hollywood to thank for this kind of thinking. A man walks on stage, hypnotizes an entire crowd, and makes them do his bidding? Given what we now know, it's highly unlikely. As I said, they need your consent.

5. Hypnosis can enhance your abilities.

That statement is somewhat true and false. Hypnosis can enhance your memory, but it can also give you false memories or distort that same memory as well. So, the results are not as significant as you would have hoped. It has also shown to be related to the enhancement of performance, but you should not expect to be running a full marathon overnight.

Now that we have looked objectively at hypnosis or what it is, I can now tell you that at the hands of a psychopath or a person with dark intentions, hypnosis can also be dangerous. Hypnosis doesn't always involve you going into a trancelike state for it to be effective. The essential elements in hypnosis are the power of suggestion and the repetitive use of words that resonates deeply with the victim. Politicians, for example, exploit this in their campaigns. They use words like change, making a difference, and so on. These words trigger a more in-depth search within one's self, and subconsciously, we find ourselves wanting that change.

You can have situations where it appears a

person becomes enthralled with another. After a few suggestions from this person, the victim rushes to do his or her bidding. In books, articles, and even in real-life situations, you often hear or read people's descriptions of a particular relationship as "being under a spell." This notion embodies the power of hypnosis and is not referring to the kind conducted on the psychologist's couch. It is more intimate, and the effect can be just as devastating. Parents have abandoned their children and given their entire wealth to a stranger because of this.

"The pendulum of the mind oscillates between sense and nonsense, not between right and wrong."

– Carl Gustav Jung

Problematic Behavior

The subject of criminal behavior is not our focus for this book, but we need to mention it because this constitutes an aspect of dark psychology. Profilers, criminologists, and law enforcement agencies benefit immensely from the study of criminal behavior. In psychology, the term criminal behavior is not often thrown around because the consensus is that crime is a behavior. However, crime engagement does not necessarily make one a criminal. Of course, there is an extensive debate on this type of thinking, but we should leave that for the experts. Our focus here is on the elements that make a person commit a crime.

Specifically, I want us to explore why people employ the use of dark psychology to hurt others. This hurt could be physical or emotional.

But before we go further into this, I call your attention to something important here.

Some people do things merely because they can, not because a troubled childhood propelled them, or because they perform vengeance for an offense they may, or may not have committed. It is in our nature to understand why. We want to make sense of our situation rather than believe that we are just victims of random acts. But we must also be prepared to consider that sometimes, the case is as it appears: a person driven by one's own personal desire to hurt others. If you bought this book seeking to find answers to questions like that, you should also open up yourself to the case that this person was just downright evil.

For a person to commit a specific type of offense, there are usually specific displayed characteristics that signify this person's capability of evil. This premise goes beyond judging a book by its cover because prolific criminals are often masters of disguises. They enchant you right before they disarm you. In our everyday lives, these people mask themselves as one of us by pretending to have our best interests at heart. Given what we now know about manipulation, deception, and hypnosis, we are aware that predators are not always strangers. So, how can you spot those things to help you make better choices in relating to people? Within this chapter, I will address five traits. As we delve more in-depth, we will explore these traits more thoroughly:

1. Family and Friends

You know that saying, show me your friends, and I would tell you who you are? Apart from yourself, examine this person's circles. Does he or she come from a close-knit family? What is his or her relationship with their family? Have you met any of their friends? If this person has no friends at all, it could be a red flag.

2. History

We like the idea of a person being wholly reformed and, in all honesty, this happens. However, you shouldn't ignore the fact that a person with a terrible history has a higher tendency to become a repeat offender. If the person was abusive in a previous relationship, there is a possibility that he or she would be the same way with you, unless the person completed or is actively undergoing treatment

3. Problems with control

People who cannot control themselves in situations that provoke them have a propensity to inflict harm on others. In the same way, people who have a problem relinquishing control can snap and lash out at the nearest victim when they lose it, and that target could be you.

4. Anti-social values

In social settings, monitor their interactions with others. People who are generally disliked by all are typically red flags. They don't have to be liked by all, but if the person is usually obnoxious, rude at getting along with people, you may have a problem on your hands.

5. Substance abuse

Dependency on any form of drug or alcohol is a clear indicator that this person is struggling with specific issues. The abuse of substance negates one's ability to reason appropriately and make sound decisions. Who abuses drugs or alcohol may not be in a position to treat your relationship as a priority in one's life. And unless this person has a way of supporting that lifestyle, you may end up paying for it directly or indirectly, which can lead to years of abuse and neglect.

These are just pointers to criminal elements in the people we relate with, but the most significant fault you can make is to see definite pointers and then rationalize them. We tend to make excuses for others. The first thing we are quick to tell ourselves is that no one is perfect. But that ideology can quickly land us in hot waters. Educate yourself, be aware, and then make informed decisions. These do not guarantee that you would be able to keep these types from hurting and taking advantage of you. But you can protect yourself from them 100% better than if you are acting from a place of ignorance.

Some of us are inherently wired to want to fix the people in our lives. We see someone who seems broken inside and think if we love them hard enough, we can bring him or her back from the brink of whatever precipice they are. From my personal experiences as well as the shared experience of others, I can confidently tell you that this is highly unlikely to work. The best-case scenario is that you become broken and spend a better part of your life healing from what you could have easily walked away from earlier.

Reverse Psychology

Technically, it is the technique to push someone, in a certain way, to do something instructing to do the opposite. For instance, if I want to convince someone to go bungy jumping without saying: do it! I could say: "I'm sure this is very complicated to do, don't jump! Only brave people can afford this experience." With a few words, I can interfere with his pride. Moreover, expertise in NLP (Neuro-Linguistic Programming) and the manipulation technique knows very well that our subconscious mind literally 'can't understand the word "don't" or "no." That means if I say: "Don't Jump," our mind will focus on the image of jumping.

For instance, if I say: Don't think about the number three. What are you thinking about right now? Your mind will focus on number 3. This technique can help us to talk and use words in a right and positive way.

Reverse psychology is a more refined form of manipulation. The main difference between reverse psychology and manipulation is that the person who ends up manipulated has an illusion of choice. He or she is made to believe that one is making a free choice, but in reality, he or she has become coerced into doing what the manipulator wants. It's enlightening when you think about the thought process that goes into pulling this off until you will find yourself as a victim.

Reverse psychology is a technique usually employed by parents in raising their children. It works well on kids who are considered "resistant" to authority. On the surface, this appears innocent with no evident harm to the child or their psyche, but it has also been well known to backfire. In our day to day activities, we use reverse psychology in our relations with others, and it is not always born from malicious intent. Let me give an example of using a wedding planner and his client.

Say this client is adamant about the choices of color to use for the wedding day. There is nothing wrong with that, but the colors in question come across as complete garish and outlandish, especially when compared with the exotic venue for the wedding and the prestigious guests invited. The wedding planner cannot tell the client one's color choices are too trashy. Instead what he does is agree with the client and then politely convey a story that hints of a very important guest who trashed a previous event because of a similar color, but then quickly adds that he is sure they can pull it off somehow. This scenario will make the client imagine the failure of the party. He will rethink the choices and voila; the planner gets what he wants in the first place.

Marketers employ this technique in selling their products to consumers as well. They agree with their consumer market on specific decisions and in acknowledging their agreement, they can convince their customers to buy their services. But parents and business owners are not the only ones guilty of using reverse psychology. We use this technique in dating as well. Most relationship experts would tell you that we are conditioned to want what we can't have. So, to make a person like you more or want you more, you make yourself unavailable to this person. It is a paradox. As with every form of reverse psychology, it can also backfire. Playing hard to get is an appeal to the human hunting instincts, but unless you plan on being elusive forever, you are going to have to stop "running." When you finish, the hunter recedes, and then you have a stalemate.

"There is nothing more deceptive than an obvious fact."

— *Arthur Conan Doyle*

Notes:

_____

_____

_____

_____

_____

_____

_____

_____

_____

_____

_____

_____

_____

_____

_____

_____

_____

_____

_____

_____

_____

_____

_____

_____

_____

_____

_____

_____

"It is during our darkest moments that we must focus to see the light.

— *Aristotle*

Chapter 4: History of persuasion

The Art of War

The strategies used in "The Art of War" can be studied and put into practice not only by great army generals, but also by managers, entrepreneurs, leaders, and politicians of every historical era, for versatility and topicality.

The art of war is between of the famous, oldest, and considered among the treaties of military writing. This book, written in the late sixth century B.C. from an anonymous Chinese person, it is attributable to the strategist of the empire Qi Sun Wu, called Sun Tzu.

The author urges an effort to achieve the maximum result with the minimum effort. He praises the general who manages to "persuade" the enemy to the point of obtaining what he wants without fighting. The first means for a valorous man is a strategic way of diplomacy, the winning weapon, getting the "perfect victory," and avoiding confrontation.

They have mainly three-ways to achieve the goals: the knowledge of the fundamental elements of war, the knowledge of oneself and the enemy, and the knowledge of the territory.

"If you know the enemy and know yourself, you need not fear the result of a hundred battles. If you know yourself but not the enemy, for every victory gained you will also suffer a defeat. If you know neither the enemy nor yourself, you will succumb in every battle."

— Sun Tzu

Those who darkly use this technique will know his victim perfectly, his strengths and weaknesses. The last chapter talks about the spy. Finding information and issuing false information: "Espionage is essential in military operations."

"Hence, it is that which none in the whole army are more intimate relations to be maintained than with spies." "None should be more liberally rewarded. In no other business should greater secrecy be preserved." Sun Tzu affirms that: "They cannot be properly managed without benevolence and straightforwardness."

The above millenary techniques can be useful in our daily life, depending on how we want to use it.

The Greek and Romans Mythology

The art of persuasion was born during the Greek domination in the fifth century B.C. in Sicily, from Corace and Tisia. Their art was continued in Athens by Trasimaco of Calcedonia and above all by Gorgia da Lentini, first recognized teacher of rhetoric and famous exponent of sophistry. He was the first philosopher to make the theory of rhetoric. He affirms that the validity of a speech depends on the "convenience" and not the integrity of its content. Speech gets manipulated from the objectives proposed by the speaker.

The Greek speaker aims to convince with the weight of arguments. The Roman speaker convinces with the weight of his authority and moral personality.

Persuading someone means influencing the mind of the interlocutor with arguments, reasons, and suggestions, so that he changes his mind about an object, a person, a political or philosophical-religious idea, etc. We often use the word to convince as if it were a synonym of persuading. Indeed, convincing means overcoming logical and rational obstacles, with methods that have the semblance of logic and rationality, to overcome resistance and doubts with the reasonable force of arguments. Persuading appeals to emotional and passional mechanisms as well as uses the same arts that we see in the seduction. Therefore, persuasion uses topics, but they are more emotional and affective than persuasive and rational. The primary weapon of persuasion is a suggestion. It is a hint orientated to condition the behavioral choice of the other person.

Aristotle

The fundamental values of human culture have remained approximately unchanged over the centuries. The foundations of effective communication were defined over 2300 years ago by the Greek philosopher Aristotle.

Aristotle's theory of persuasion is part of more significant work in three books written around 350 B.C.

According to Aristotle, persuasion is an art:

It is the art of persuading people to do specific actions that they would not normally do if we did not ask them to do them.

The great philosopher observed that, as social animals, we are called almost daily to persuade others. We are leading the interlocutor (or the public) from the starting point A to the end of arrival, point B (the objective).

Aristotle pointed out the three fundamental factors on which the persuasive speaker can leverage to make his speech convincing:

• Ethos (ethics, moral strength, and the reputation of the speaker);

• Pathos (emotionality, the ability to appeal to feelings);

• Logos (logic).

The messages that are most effective in their persuasive intent are those that lead the interlocutor from point A to point B using the three elements together.

Ethos

The Ethos concerns the speaker and the moral strength he communicates. The verbal message is credible only if the source from which it comes is credible.

The speaker should gain credibility in the mind of the public.

Pathos

Pathos is related to the emotions felt by the public. According to Aristotle, the speech can convince the listener if it arouses emotions in him. To be persuasive, the speaker must rely on the feelings of the public, with empathy.

Logos

The logos refers to the verbal discourse, to the words spoken by the speaker. Aristotle emphasized the importance of constructing discourse with the most appropriate words and enriching it with anecdotes, quotations, and examples.

According to Aristotle, the most critical factor for persuasion was the logos, while he attributed a secondary role to ethos and pathos.

Accordingly, with James Borg, author of "The Art of Influencing People," today there are valid reasons to recognize the priority of the ethos, followed by pathos, and therefore by logos.

Let us think about the importance of trust (ethos) in our daily lives. For instance, if we discover that politicians are liars or that they didn't keep their promises, we no longer believe what they say, even if they use pathos (emotions) and logos (logic)

This rule, of course, could be applied to all kinds of our relationships.

Aristotle explained that to persuade others, we must resort to a set of logic and emotion. So the persuasive process works on two levels, which we call consciousness and subconscious.

Logic is about consciousness. The interlocutor evaluates intellectually and then rationally decides whether the topic convinces him or not.

Someone instead let themselves be guided more by the subconscious. They evaluate the information exposed by the "persuader" intuitively with the emotions they arouse in them.

Even if we are logical and very aware people,

we let ourselves be guided mainly by instinct. Logic, however, is fundamental, because it is the element that helps us to validate the decision we have made; and this is indispensable because emotions can be fleeting.

Sigmund Freud

Sigmund Freud was a medical neurologist and founder of psychoanalysis. Freud is known to have developed the psychoanalytic theory that unconscious psychic processes influence thought, human behavior, and interactions between individuals. Starting from medical education, he tried to establish correlations between the vision of the unconscious, symbolic representation of real processes, and its components with the physical structures of the mind and the human body.

In 1921 Freud published a booklet, of about a hundred pages, called Group Psychology and the Analysis of the Ego. That was a period of severe economic crisis and a period in which organized workers' struggles were born, the great ideologies, the dictatorships. In Italy, the National Fascist Party and the Italian Communist Party were born, while in Germany Adolf Hitler became the leader of the National Socialist Party German. Freud studied the mass's behavior intensely, facing up to sociological issues in a psychoanalytic key. Freud began to reflect on collective psychology, trying to show that the phenomena that regulate group life are not any different from psychoanalytic discoveries related to individual processes. There are two types of the masses: the first one is occasional, transient, unorganized, such as trends. The other one is an organized, permanent end enduring mass.

The mass is destined to last longer, such as the church and the army. The "soul of the mass" is therefore described as elementary and passionate, prone to illusions, since the Overself is temporarily set aside, to the advantage of a quasi-hypnotic bond, which triggers impulses, losing the critical spirit, feeling a sense of omnipotence and impunity. Individuals who are part of a mass, therefore, lose autonomy and balance but acquire the feeling of being active, as part of an organized whole, which reassures and protects. The mass is changeable, impulsive, irritable, and, being governed entirely by the unconscious, it does not tolerate any delay between the desire and the realization of that desire. After all, none of what the masses do is intentional. They experience a narcissistic regression, with the disappearance of all personal inhibitions, in favor of instincts, entirely out of control. It is not so uncommon for the mass to perform cruel acts, such as lynching, but also acts of extreme generosity, overcoming the limits imposed by the need for self-preservation.

Sigmund Freud's ideas on the unconscious mind were used by the powerful to control the masses in post-war America.

Politicians and planners came to believe that Freud's conclusions were right, that hidden in the depths of the human being, there would be dangerous and irrational desires and fears.

They were convinced that the release of these instincts had led to barbarism and Nazism in Germany.

To prevent it from happening again, they tried to find ways to control this enemy within the human mind.

The protagonists of this story are the daughter of Sigmund Freud, Anna and his nephew Edward Bernays, the inventor of public relations.

Their ideas got used by the U.S. government, the business community, and the CIA to develop techniques to control and manage the minds of American citizens.

The Government believed that the only way democracy could work and create a stable society was to suppress the savage barbarism that existed just below the surface of ordinary life.

The Jungian Shadow

Everyone claims to know themselves well, but just how true is that?

Fair enough, we all have a good knowledge of our values, opinions, belief systems, and desires as well as specific codes of conduct. We abide by which determines whether or not we are the "good" guys, and that counts as something, too. True. But is this really all there is to us we that we know?

If there is one person we know better than anyone else in the world, it is ourselves, surely. But what if we don't even know ourselves enough to know we know nothing?

What if a whole bunch of information we have about ourselves is nothing but a sham, and our beliefs and desires and morality are an inaccurate depiction of our true selves?

While pondering on that thought still, let's try to recall the many different times we have acted on impulse and gone on to regret our actions and berate ourselves.

And sometimes, our impulses were justifiable, but somehow, we had started to regret our actions like it wasn't us performing the regrettable action a while ago. We attribute that impulsive action to a lack of self-control and momentary madness, but what if in truth, it was another "us" skulking behind the careful construct of what we perceive ourselves to be?

Every story has a villain and a hero. What if we play both roles in our own story? Incredulous, right? Well, it's not so much compared to how we were performing an action one minute and regretting it the next.

The good and bad aspects of our lives constitute the story of our personalities. A story that we have to know and understand before any other person. But to follow this story, we must learn to perceive. To be aware of our desires and fears; because try as we might try to shut off our concerns and darkness in willful ignorance, they are part of us. There is no issue in trying to shy away from them, something that is innate in us for a long time and will always be.

But what is this part of us? Meet the Shadow.

Carl Gustav Jung, the Swiss psychiatrist, is

credited with the coinage of the context of a shadow identity. And it was no unintentionally or ordinary naming.

The use of the word Shadow in this context points to Jung's way of demonstrating a complex idea in a manner that is capable of being understood and imagined.

In Jungian psychology, the shadow identity definition is the unconscious aspect of the human personality, which is not identified by the conscious ego. Another definition regards it as a sum of the unconscious, that is, all areas of the nature of which people are not well aware; hence, it is unconscious. In all, the shadow identity is simply the unknown side of the personality fraction.

Since we are all wired to turn down or remain willfully ignorant of the unwanted parts of our personalities, the shadow identity is deemed to be mainly negative. Albeit, there are sometimes positive aspects that remain hidden in the shadow I.D.; particularly in people who have anxieties, fake belief systems, and poor self-esteem.

Contrary to the Freudian description of the shadow I.D., in Jungian psychology, the Shadow can comprise every personality trait beyond the sphere of conscious thought and may be manifested as good or evil.

The Shadow could well be the connection to a more primitive animal instinct in humans, one which is superseded by the conscious mind during the period of early childhood.

It is these projections that are capable of harming and insulting people by acting as the ever-thickening veil of illusion inhibiting the ego from the real world.

Any area of the unconscious identity, which is unable to metamorphose into conscious perception, will continuously inhibit progress as it creates a fictitious world, this is unable to sync with the frequencies of the real world. In this regard, the real world, as one perceives it, becomes a battleground of egotism, which results in insanity and collision. That is no progressive way for both perceptions to meet. The word should be neutral ground for regular experimentation and dialogue where we put great efforts into refining the essential morals which could alleviate our sufferings. Anything outside of this is skepticism, and if it seems rather too sharp for some people, it is proof that the shadow identity does not get adequately addressed.

The Appearance of the shadow identity

The shadow identity could appear in visions and dreams taking on different forms. However, it usually appears as an individual of the same gender as the dreamer. Carl Jung also suggested that there is more than one layer that makes up the Shadow. The top layers of the Shadow have the exhibition and meaningful flow of personal experiences. These factors are often unconscious to an individual owing to alterations in attention, willful repression, or simple forgetfulness. However, beneath all these idiosyncrasies are the archetypes that constitute the mental aspect of every human experience.

Origins of the Shadow

Society has instilled in us over time that certain attitudes about lifestyle choices, sexual desires, emotional patterns, etc. are inappropriate. However, it is these improper factors that serve to disrupt the functional flow of society, even though the disruption would involve making people accept things they would find uncomfortable. Anyone who seems a little too challenging outrightly becomes an outcast, and others move on. Humans are generally social creatures. This reason accounts for the phenomenology of the population. So, people exist as a group in a specific location. By the idea of our social quality, the one thing we have come to dread is getting excommunicated from the lot.

This argument proves that for each time we cross the line, as we almost always do religiously, the repercussions of our actions are meted out on us. People will not fail to condemn, judge, or gossip about us. The accompanying emotion, although unpleasant in itself, can become overwhelming.

We don't need other people to perceive our deviance to get affected by it. Eventually, we end up inflicting the backlash of society on ourselves by internalizing it deeply. The only way to go out of this never-ending pain is to masquerade it. Step into the ego. We always chide ourselves about who we are not, who we are, and the lengths to which we could go to prevent the possibility of becoming an outcast from ever happening.

It is a somewhat correct assumption to say that just about everyone possesses a quality that doesn't quite sit well with society and is termed undesirable. Society says that the perfect or ideal individual is nonexistent because one would have to live up to impossible standards indeed.

Characteristics of the Shadow identity

1. Playing the victim every time:

Instead of admitting to wrongdoing, people will sometimes go all the way to deny involvement by describing themselves to be an innocent passerby. If anything, these people hate to take responsibility.

2. Highlighting one's insecurities as flaws in others:

Internet is one of the most popular places to host this. Scan through some comments and posts, and you will see internet trolls who insult and throw shade at both the commenter and author. Ironically, some of the most insecure people are internet trolls.

3. The tendency to judge others harshly and on impulse:

We sometimes find ourselves pointing out to a friend how ridiculing someone else looked. We wouldn't like to get called out this way, so being the one doing the calling out seems to reassure you that you know better than to make the same mistakes as the person.

4. Stepping over others for selfish gains:

As much as people celebrate their successes,

they rarely ever give cognizance to the many different times; they cheated others to achieve their success. A typical scenario on a small scale is how people vie for positions on the freeway and make it by cutting off others in traffic. On a large scale, consider how political parties rig elections to ensure their candidates attain the seat of power.

5. Quick temper with people in subservient positions:

This factor is prevalent in the relationship between customers and customer service employees. People have no problem in developing an attitude for people with limited or no power. Exercising power over others is the way the Shadow compensates for the feeling of helplessness one experiences when faced with a greater force.

"Everything that irritates us about others can lead us to an understanding of ourselves."
– Carl G. Jung

Notes:

_____
_____
_____
_____
_____
_____
_____
_____
_____
_____
_____
_____
_____
_____
_____
_____
_____
_____
_____
_____
_____
_____
_____
_____
_____
_____
_____
_____

"Never attempt to win by force what can be won by deception."

— *Niccolò Machiavelli*

Chapter 5: The dark triad

The dark triad may sound like something out of a Hollywood movie, but it is the cornerstone of dark psychology and, by extension, this book. It refers to the three personality types that inspired the inception of dark psychology.

The dark triad consists of Machiavellianism, Narcissism, and Psychopathy.

There are some differences between the three psychological concepts contained in the dark triad. See the explanations below.

Machiavellianism is all about manipulation and deceit, manipulating people to get what you want. People associate Machiavellianism with a political type who took the book 'The Prince' a little too seriously;

Narcissism is all about admiration and believing that you should get treated like royalty or something, enamored with their image;

Psychopathy is all about being insensitive and cold to others and their needs. They may look like someone straight out of a slasher film.

The real-life examples of these traits are more sinister than that as they can easily slip under the radar and operate under the veil of the general public ignorance.

The dark triad is associated with personality traits that show an active link to Borderline Personality Disorder (BPD). Someone could manifest just one of the qualities represented in the dark triad. Unfortunately, the worst case will be when someone reveals a high concentration of one part of the combination of the triad.

We will go further to discuss these separately and at length.

Narcissism

Narcissism is one of the personality traits which comprises the dark triad. It refers to a longing for self-gratification, usually from egoistical adoration of one's pristine qualities and self-image or other vain sources.

In 1914, Sigmund Freud's essay On Narcissism classified Narcissism as a concept of psychoanalytic theory. In 1968 it was classified as a personality disorder and listed in the DSM (Diagnostic and Statistical Manual of Mental Disorders) from the American Psychiatric Association based firmly on the concept of historical megalomania.

By and large, Narcissism is a cultural and social issue. It is one of the many factors of the trait theory used in different self-reported inventories on a personality like the Millon Clinical Multiaxial Inventory. Narcissism is regarded as a problem in the relationship of a group or individual with themselves and others when it is not in its primary form otherwise considered as healthy self-love. Throughout the years, many different schools of thought have linked Narcissism to egocentrism, but the truth remains that both concepts, although similar in some contexts, are distinct in themselves.

Origin of Narcissism

The word "Narcissism" is of Greek coinage. The word so comes about from Greek mythology about a youth named Narcissus or Narkissos in Greek. By the account of Ovid, he was handsome and pleasant to behold, earning him the love of the nymph, Echo. Countlessly did Narcissus turn down the advances of Echo, choosing instead to gaze upon a reflection of his image in a pool of water. And so, it happened that young Narcissus became enamored and loved the image of himself reflected in the body of water. Albeit, being unable to consummate his newfound love, young Narcissus laid by the pool for hours unending, entranced by the reflection of his image. Finally, he turned into a flower which till today is called after him, the Narcissus.

Throughout history, the concept of extreme selfishness gets mentioned a lot, in historical Greece, the theory is synonymous with the term' hubris.' It wasn't until recently that Narcissism began defined in terms of psychology.

Narcissistic Personality Disorder (NPD)

A narcissistic personality disorder is related to a type of dramatic personality disorder characterized by a distorted image of self.

The National Library Of Medicine of the USA defines people diagnosed with a narcissistic personality disorder as ones exhibiting excessive preoccupation of self, apathy towards other people, and an overly construed feeling of self-importance. That is, individuals who get diagnosed with NPD tend to have intense and unstable emotions as well as extravagant yearnings for power, vanity, individual capability, and prestige. Such people have lower chances of exhibiting empathy and a higher tendency to show a hyperbolic sense of superiority. Studies suggest that such extremity in feelings and concerns could be a result of the lack of self-confidence, self-esteem, and insecurity.

NPD is a character trait linked to egocentrism — a behavioral pattern in which persons consider themselves and their concerns as superior to that of others. Thus, people with NPD tend to have no interest in the welfare of others, showing a great deal of apathy, which makes them indifferent to the emotions not related to them.

Dimensions of Narcissism

As a personality variable, there are four significant dimensions of Narcissism, including:

1. Superiority and arrogance.
2. Exploitativeness and entitlement.
3. Leadership and authority.
4. Absorption and self-admiration.

Characteristics and Traits of Narcissism

The outline below is some of the prevalent traits that define Narcissism:

1. Taking advantage of others to achieve an aim without regret or respect for their feelings.
2. Insatiable longing for attention.
3. Haughty and arrogant behavior.
4. Ostentatious, egotistical, and boastful.
5. Excessive jealousy, especially when not the center of attraction.
6. Envying and believing to be envied.
7. Expectations of special treatment and favor.
8. Yearning for loyal compliance with all expectations.
9. Exaggerating self-worth, talents, and

accomplishments.

10. Apathy or indifference, and disregard for the emotions of others.

11. An exaggerated sense of one's romantic skills.

12. A sensitive attitude to criticism.

13. Easily prompted to feel hurt or rejected with little provocation.

14. A near inability to maintain relationships for long durations.

15. A negative response to criticisms, shame, and humiliation.

16. Seeking extolment from others.

17. Conditioned to expect positive reinforcements from other people.

18. Fantasizing about one's success, appearance, intelligence, and power.

19. Insistence on being served the best and nothing less.

20. Believing very few others understand one's peculiarity.

21. Believing to be superior.

22. Belittling others who are considered inferior.

23. Monopolizing conversations and attention.

24. Hyperbolic sense of self-worth.

25. Relating only to others who are perceived

to be equally superior.

26. An exaggerated feeling of entitlement.

The seven deadly sins of Narcissism

The seven deadly sins of Narcissism, developed by two psychiatrists; James F. Masterson and Hotchkiss, includes the following list:

1. Arrogance:

It is very much like narcissists who feel deflated to re-inflate their feeling of self-worth by degrading, diminishing, and debasing other people.

2. Magic Thinking:

Narcissists consider themselves no short of perfect, using distorted and illusive self-images. The whole process of thinking and imagining themselves this way, termed as magical thinking, is also defined as this such thinking allows them to project shame on other people.

3. Sense of entitlement:

It is only normal for narcissists to have quite unreasonable expectations of anyone. They expect to be given special treatment and have all their needs met without questions because they think of themselves as more superior and unique. When people fail to do their biddings, narcissists consider their superiority challenged, and the challenger gets labeled as difficult or awkward. Defying their will is narcissistic damage, which is capable of activating narcissistic rage.

4. Shamelessness:

Shamelessness is just another tick in the day for the Narcissist, so it is no doubt how open and proud they are about it. Since they are generally an apathetic lot with no concern whatsoever for the feelings of others, narcissists hate getting shamed. They regard shame as a toxic quality, which demonstrates just how imperfect and in need of change they are.

Thus, narcissists would rather be guilty than shamed; because the former allows them the room to sever anything connecting them to their actions. Meaning their intentions are good even though the accompanying actions seemed wrong.

5. Poor Boundaries:

Narcissists do not grasp the basic concept of boundaries. They fail to understand how much of a limit inhibits them from interfering with other people's lives. Narcissists barely understood the fact that other people are distinct entities and not mere extensions of themselves. They figure other people exist to do their biddings or may not have existed at all.

In a narcissist's mind, there is barely any noticeable boundary between themselves and others.

6. Envy:

Narcissists can find the feeling of superiority when faced by the ability of others by employing contempt in belittling others and their accomplishments.

7. Exploitation:

Narcissists are capable of taking on many different forms. However, the result is always the same in the case of exploitation because they carry it out without consideration of the emotions and interests of others. Often, they are exploitive of persons in subservient positions where resistance is either too difficult to achieve or an impossible feat altogether.

Albeit, the subservience is frequently not as real as they assume, causing the exploitation process to birth many different relationship spells, which are both brief and short-lived.

Symptoms of Narcissism

Although the various types of Narcissism have symptoms peculiar to their different contexts, some symptoms are synonymous to them all.

Such symptoms are inclusive but not limited to, the following:

1. Narcissistic people are prone to becoming angry and impatient when they do not seem to be special by others, as they deem themselves.

2. People who exhibit Narcissism will often have interpersonal issues, which makes them prone to being difficult.

3. Another common symptom of Narcissism is disdain and fury. Narcissists almost always try to demean other people because they believe themselves to be superior.

4. Lack of control over their behavior and emotions.

5. Narcissists may sometimes fall into a state

of depression or moodiness, especially when they find out about imperfections or shortcomings on their part.

6. Narcissistic people experience a significant challenge in adapting to new conditions and dealing with stress.

7. Narcissists are quite prone to nursing silent fears of vulnerability, insecurity, embarrassment, and inferiority.

Causes of Narcissism

There is no definite factor that can be ascribed as the cause of Narcissism because there are, in fact, lots of factors that can trigger it. As it is with behavioral patterns, the reason of Narcissism is likely complicated. However, some of the known factors that can trigger Narcissism include the following:

1. Innateness:

It is safe to say that everyone person has a tinge of Narcissism in them. This factor, however, refers to the right or positive variant of Narcissism associated with self-love.

2. Environmental factors:

The environment can affect the way a person exhibits narcissistic behavior. Any mismatch in the parent(s)–child(ren) relationship characterized by excessive criticism or adoration can constitute how narcissistic a person can turn out. For instance, if a child gets abused or neglected, has over-pampering parents, or parents with high expectations, chances are the child could end up being a narcissist.

3. Genetical factors:

Studies show that NPD (narcissistic personality disorder) can be an inherited trait in people. The same is true for Narcissism. After all, the pear doesn't fall far from the tree. A person can sometimes become narcissistic by learning the behavior of manipulation from their parents or guardians, siblings, or relatives while growing.

4. Biological factors:

Sometimes, the connection between the way the brain functions, the manner of thinking, and the behavioral pattern of a person can be a causal factor. For instance, if people that get taught vulnerability is an unacceptable quality, their ability to understand and be empathetic to the needs and feelings of other people can be hindered. In this vein, what they learned has influenced their perception and behavior.

Machiavellianism

One of the best quotes we could use to identify the Machiavellism behavior is: "The Ends Justify the Means." Like all three of the personality types on the dark triad, the Machiavellian is often insanely charming. They know how exactly to charm their way into or around any social situation to get what they want. All that counts for them is that they get what they want by any means necessary.

Machiavellianism refers to a behavioral pattern characterized by deceit, cynical perceptions towards the nature of man, manipulativeness, and an aloof, calculating attitude towards other people.

The term Machiavellianism traces its origin to Niccolò Machiavelli, an Italian philosopher, and diplomat after which it became conceptualized. Machiavelli lived through the Renaissance era as one of the finest and well-known writers. His book, Il Principe, translated as "The Prince" in

English, is the most popular of his writings owing to the oddity of Machiavelli's ideology.

While imprisoned, he wrote a book detailing all the principles he deemed necessary for rulers and would-be rulers to acquire and retain power. He sent the book to the ruler in the hopes that it would buy him some boon in the eyes of the "Prince" De Medici.

This book became the blueprint used by politicians and those who might rule over people in a broad and impactful fashion. While most people have some of these Machiavellian traits, they will seldom act on them too often. The true Machiavellian does not care about moderating these behaviors. They will live by them as if by some philosophical code for their lives.

The book encouraged Machiavelli's opinion on strong leadership, where he opined that influential leaders should rule both their enemies and subjects with an iron fist. He went on to state that survival and glory were justifiable by all means, including the ones that would otherwise be considered brutal and immoral.

What Machiavelli implied was that leaders should do anything to get what they wanted regardless of the costs.

From some recent studies, there is proof that

he never pronounces the popular notion "the Ends Justify the Means." Regardless of who wrote it, the quote is helpful to understand the Machiavellian behavior better clearly.

It is relevant to highlight that this is one of the most natural traits for people to adopt and benefit from, despite being a symptom of mental illness. People can be born with this trait, though, but the evidence that supports this is rare. People high in Machiavellianism (high Machs) get subjected to a childhood that involved a cold style of parenting.

High Machs are master manipulators capable of ruining the lives of many while having the potential to teach many about those who play games of power and how to handle yourself around them. It does not matter whether one intends to learn about them out of curiosity; these people offer a lot of wisdom to offer anyone willing to learn.

How does the High Mach operate?

They can be selfish people with very little or no sense of morality or remorse.

One of the examples to conjure up this person

is the character, Iago, from Shakespeare's "Othello." High Machs, like Iago, are cunning and very manipulative, using anyone or anything to help them get the advantages they want and feel they deserve. They will cunningly operate from the shadows and show surprising amounts of patience because the result matters more than anything else to them. The only thing that might matter as much as the final result to a High Mach is their reputation.

Reputation to someone high in Machiavellianism is king. There is no better way of not getting caught out as a deceiving manipulator than having a pristine reputation. Think of politicians or business people who get found out for having been involved in some scandalous affair or dodgy dealing long after they were dead or retired. These are the kinds of people who hid their sordid personas behind the impeccable reputation. Machiavellians tend to be drawn to the long game because they often consider their goals more important than human relationships. They don't feel any personal attachments to hold them back.

High Machs are often so dedicated to their interests that people around them only exist on two sides of the same coin: those who benefit me and those who do not. People are just a tool for them to use and manipulate to their end. If you get in their way through, they will deal with you ruthlessly as they have no remorse and are cynical by nature, because they don't believe in any inherent goodness in people.

What can we learn from Machiavellians?

While most people might not be high in trait Machiavellianism, there is a lot we can learn from this leg of the dark triad. Ordinary people can learn from Machiavellian in some way so that they can live more peaceful lives if not even take advantage of them. That last part speaks more to people who are very low on the Machiavellian scale and tend to be too 'nice' or agreeable.

The potential to build a better life in many respects is found in this part of the dark triad if one knows what to look out for and use wisely. There are many bad aspects to being a high Mach, but there are some significant advantages to being willing to learn from this type of person. In the end, one should be able to know enough to identify if they are part of some elaborate game that they might be forced to pay for later on.

Patience and reputation are among the most significant things one can take away from the Machiavellian. Loathed to investing in short cuts, the Machiavellian teaches us that patience is vital when climbing the ladder of power and success. They behave like predators, claws, and teeth ever ready to strike in an instant, but patiently waiting for the right situation to pounce while concealing themselves as they wait.

People are also means, so learning how to pick and choose the right targets so that they rise to the top is made faster is crucial. Though, the best way to attain that trust is to make sure that one's reputation is kept spotless. If something underhanded has to happen, then find someone to do it for you while you keep your nose clean. A good reputation will do a lot of your persuading for you.

Machiavellianism is often depicted in behavior by shallow affectations as well as a low level of emotional attachment to other people. Machiavellians also tend to be quite concentrated in themselves while approaching life with a selfish focus. They also exhibit apathetic qualities and have little to no atom of humility and honesty in them.

The origin of Machiavellianism studies

The behavioral model was conceived into a concept by Geiss and Christie in the year 1970; Although the origins of Machiavellianism in behavior isn't exactly clear, research has shown that it is innate, meaning Machiavellianism may well be in the genetics. According to other studies, Machiavellianism can also stem from a bad start to life, especially from younger ages.

If a child is sexually harassed, orphaned, or moved from one foster home to another at a young age, the said child could grow up with traits of Machiavellianism in their personality.

What drives Machiavellianism?

The answer is power. Researches made in current times have concluded that the primary motive behind Machiavellianism is the hunger for power. Let's consider how these fit in with the definition of Machiavellianism which gets described as a personality trait possessed by a person so focused on their interests that they manipulate, exploit and even deceive to get what they want — power.

A typical example of Machiavellians is politicians. Mainly, politicians are believed to be Machiavellians because they manipulate, exploit, and lie to achieve selfish interests. Their selfishness is what makes them a rather dangerous lot. Machiavellians believe that whoever wields absolute power, be it financial or positional, dictates how things happen.

Characteristics of Machiavellism:

1. Struggling to decipher their emotions.

Most Machiavellians have a hard time understanding their emotions. Most of them cannot even identify them talk more about understanding them. Instead of trying, they just shut their feelings out. That is why people would consider Machiavellians as entirely heartless. They get what they want by any means necessary without looking back. Shutting their emotions out enables them to act the way they do.

2. Manipulate others to go forward.

Machiavellians are very good at manipulating people to get what they want. It might be power, money, respect; you name it. If they want it, they will surely get it by any means necessary, even if it means manipulating and exploiting anybody at any time. They are so good at managing people to the extent that the people that get manipulated have no idea that they are getting deceived.

3. It can cause harm to get what they want.

A Machiavellian can do anything to get what they want, as we all know. But anything like what? They can resort to lying, killing, or even kidnapping to get what they want. They have no empathy to worry about the consequences of their actions. They have it in mind that the end justifies the means. They don't care how they get there; all they want to do is get there.

4. It doesn't make you aware of the consequences of their actions.

Some Machiavellians are aware of the consequences of their actions, while others are not. They don't want to know the consequences of their actions. All they want to know is how they will get to where they want to be. All they care about is reaching for that power that they want so bad. They don't care if the consequences of their actions could cost a life or more. They believe that attaining power and money is the only thing that would get them all they want on earth.

5. Low levels of sympathy.

Just like other personality traits in the dark triad, this personality trait also shows a low level of sympathy towards people. A Machiavellian has little or no empathy for anyone. They never feel remorse or guilt for whatever they do at any time. All they care about is themselves.

Machiavellians usually believe that, if they let empathy into the equation, it will slow them down and distract them from the real thing that they want to achieve: money, power, or respect.

6. They usually flatter a lot.

These people with this particular trait have a way of getting what they want. One of those ways is flattery. They can sweet talk anyone to do anything. They will gratify you and tell you what you want to hear just because they want something from you. They can spend the whole day trying to sweet talk you into getting what they want. In most of the case, they are so smart to the make you do what he wants, and you not even know that you ended up persuaded through flattery.

7. They are always in disguise.

How?

They never tend to show their true intentions. You can be with a Machiavellian for a very long time. We are talking about being with them for years, and you might not be able to know their true intentions completely. They are very good at masking or disguising their true intentions. They do this because they never want to reveal the real purpose and blowing their cover.

8. They always avoid commitments or even emotional attachments.

By now, we all know the kind of people Machiavellians are, but you should also know that they don't like commitments or emotional attachments. They find it challenging to maintain a steady relationship with anyone. They would prefer to be alone all their life as far as they get what they want. If you see a Machiavellian who is so committed to a particularly emotional relationship, you should know that he or she is up to something cynical. If pretending to like someone is going to get them what they want, they are ready to do it for as long as they can.

9. They are very patient and calculative.

These types of people have a way of setting plans in motion and letting it work in their favor. They can only do this with a very high level of patience. Machiavellians can calculate how long it would take them to get to a particular state or political power in life. After doing that, they can set certain things in motion and watch it unfold slowly and steadily to their advantage. They never seem to be in haste. All they know is that at the end of it all they would surely get what exactly they are want.

10. They are good at reading social conditions or situations.

Someone understanding large crowds is another way you can quickly identify a Machiavellian. They have an idea of reading and understanding a social situation. This ability comes as a result of them being able to control a huge crowd. Many of them use this ability to access their different means of manipulation because they know that you cannot use the same means of manipulation for everybody. Some people are just wired differently from others, so they try their best to read you and understand what kind of manipulation technique would be best.

These characteristics of Machiavellianism are as good as they come. They should be able to effectively help you identify a Machiavellian and understand his or her actual motives no matter how small. Machiavellians are everywhere, sometimes we see them but do not know who they are. With these characteristics, you would not only spot them in a crowd; you will also be able to understand their every move and or motive.

This particular personality trait is one that is cold and straight forward. It is one of the deadliest amongst the dark triad. It gives a person the ability to be mischievous and deceitful. Many Machiavellians can be very cunning. That is why most Machiavellians are said to be in politics. Most politicians would tell you what you want to hear for you to give them exactly what they want, which is power and respect. When you believe them and vote for them, you help them get closer to their goals. There have been thousands of reports of politicians not fulfilling their promises immediately that they get that power.

That is one of the points why politicians are not to be trusted. There is a high possibility that 70% of politicians are Machiavellians.

Machiavellians are not able to keep commitments. They don't want anything that would tie them down for a very long time. Even if they get married, they would still act like they have no wife. They don't want anything that would hinder their ambitions or their goals

And the moment you try to meddle in their affairs, they are going to throw you out of their lives as quickly as you got in.

You should be careful with Machiavellians because they can be very deceitful, they can control two personas at a time. Some of them could manage multiple personalities, and you would never be able to find out who they are. Some people make reports of people they used to know that changed very fast. You would think that everybody changes, but you should be aware of the likelihood that the person is a Machiavellian.

There are some differences between the three psychological concepts contained in the dark triad. They get discussed below.

Machiavellianism is all about manipulation and deceit, manipulating people to get what you want.

Narcissism is all about admiration and believing that you should need treatment like royalty or something.

Psychopathy is all about being insensitive and cold to others and their needs.

They are very deadly in their ways. If you have, as a family member, friend, or mere acquaintance, anyone who displays any of these personality traits should make you tread with caution. They can be so caring, and extremely understanding, but are, ultimately, very dangerous.

What Are The Causes Of Machiavellianism?

There are different causes of Machiavellianism, and we will talk about just a few that can be very easy to recognize, especially at a young age.

These causes include:

1. Moving from foster home to foster home.

If a child is moved from foster home to foster home from when he or she is a baby to when he or she is 11, there is a huge possibility that the person could be a Machiavellian.

How do we help?

Take some of them off the street or from a foster home. Teach them the importance of feelings and emotions, tell them what to do and how to do it. Make them your friend. Show them how a lovely home should look, and most importantly, make sure they make good friends.

2. Divorce.

When parents get separated (divorce), it always has a way of affecting their child or children. Especially if the parents start sharing the time they spend with the children. When a child misses his mom or dad and can't get to them, it could bring the idea that they are alone. And that they have no other person in the world to tell what's bothering them. The worst thing you can do in a divorce is to shield yourself and your emotions from your children. Some of the children could generate a method to survive the lack of attention from their parents. The children could start using some tactics to take advantage of the situation. It could look hard to admit that our children are using dark behavior, but it is better to recognize it and take immediate action.

How do you help?

Make sure that you have a good and functional relationship with your children even after divorce. It would help your children feel more at ease and less alone. Dysfunctional homes bring about the dark triad's personality traits. When children don't have a lovely home to thrive in, they think of other ways to feel important in the world. That is where those personality traits start kicking in. And you should believe that if you are not able to do something about it when they are young, it will be much more difficult to do anything about it when they are older, especially when they are teens.

The Machiavellian test.

In this test, different people get 100 questions to answer. If they score above 60, they are considered to be high MACHS, and if they score below 60, they are considered to be low MACHS.

High MACHS are people that care about the wellbeing of only themselves. They believe that, like them, one must be deceitful to get ahead in life.

Low MACHS is the exact opposite of high MACHS. They believe in empathy, they have remorse, and they don't think that power and money are everything. And most importantly, most low MACHS put the needs of others before their own.

In conclusion, Machiavellianism is a personality trait that is hard to understand and spot. You should also know that if you take care of the situation when a Machiavellian is still young, you could tend to avoid an impending catastrophe.

Psychopathy

Psychopathy is one of the three personality traits in the dark triad.

When we talk about psychopathy, the mind could quickly fly to serial killers, heinous crimes, and 'Hannibal Lecter.' In this book, we will focus more on the one that remains outside prison.

Psychopathy could refer to mental illness or disorder. In the dark triad, it can be a lack of sympathy and self-control. It gets considered as the malicious and spiteful of the dark triad — people who are considered psychopathic exhibit low sympathy and also show high levels of unpredictable behavior.

As a part of the dark triad personality, it can

be harmful in any area of a person's life. Be it work, school, church, or even at home. Research shows that people that exhibit these traits may be highly skilled and highly orientated as the case may be.

There are also other researches which state that the dark triad personalities can be shown or seen on the faces of people. But during these researches, scientists found out that they could only decipher Narcissism in the faces of people, but Machiavellianism and psychopathy were almost impossible to spot and or read in the faces of people. The question is, are they that complex? The answer is a big yes. Those two unidentified traits are the most difficult to decipher, although further researches have gone into finding ways to spot these characteristics on the faces of people.

People that exhibit the psychopathy personality are complicated to understand because they always have a way of getting out of any circumstance. You can ask a psychopath a direct question, and he/she will only tell you what they want you to know and not what you want to know. It is somewhat impossible to get forcefully get information from the head of a psychopath.

Identifying people with dark triad traits is probably one of the most challenging things to do. But there is some subtle sign that you can notice in people for you to have a slight or brief knowledge of who they are. It is essential to keep in mind that these methods are experimental and have not been thoroughly tested and confirmed, so you must be cautious.

Without further hesitation, some of the ways of identifying or detecting the psychopathic personality traits of a person are by observing some of the following:

1. They tend to be cynical.

First of all, a cynical person is one who distrusts everyone and believes that their self-esteem motivates people. In other words, they are concerned with only their interests, disregarding the benefit of others. They doubt almost everybody around them.

2. These people lack remorse.

Remorse is one the main thing that makes us human beings, and if you don't have that, you are pretty much not a complete human being. Remorse is when a person has sincere regret for a wrong committed.

Psychopaths do not exhibit this particular trait. Even if they have remorse, it would be so small, so that you could not notice it. They believe that showing remorse makes them weak and vulnerable to the bad things of the world. Joined with the fact that they trust nobody, they also don't have remorse for any of their actions.

3. They tend to exploit others.

They tend to get things from people without giving anything in return. It makes them who they are. They do unbelievable things, and this is one of them. They take advantage of people just for their amusement. People should be afraid of psychopaths because they can make you do things even you don't normally do. They have a twisted mind, and they can twist your mind to do what they want you to do. You can try and resist, but as long as you are close to them, they will eventually get inside your head.

4. They don't care about what the world think about them.

Psychopathy is a strange phenomenon. These people are very different from others, as we all know. Some of them don't think that they are part of this world. They have a mindset that the world is full of evil and bad people. That is why most psychopaths talk less and do more. They are especially uncomfortable in social situations and would always seek out. They believe that the people in the world are not worthy enough to associate with them. The bottom line is that they don't take care of what the world thinks about them.

5. They are particularly insensitive.

Insensitivity means showing no care or concern for the feelings of people. Psychopaths show no responsibility or worry about other people's opinions. They can see a person crying and walk away. They have little or absolutely no concern for the feelings of other people.

They can be so insensitive to the extent that they see it as a regular thing, despite the implications of their actions.

6. They tend to be good at lying.

A psychopath can lie to get out of any situation. They can tell you a lie in a way that it becomes the truth to you. They twist your mind into believing them. Some of them are called psychopathic liars. You cannot get any truthful information from them. They will know the truth. They are conscious of the fact, but they choose to lie. They prefer lying to get out of a situation order than telling the truth and just getting over with it.

People that exhibit these types of behaviors tend towards being a psychopath as relates to the concept of the dark triad. If you live with people like this, the only thing you can do is to keep an open mind. Never let them change what you believe, and most importantly, never let them get into your head. If they do, it will be tough for you to remove them and, before you know it, you are becoming more like them without you even knowing. So, let them be as much as you can.

Psychopathy makes them believe that this world is full of evil. So how do psychopaths process that? They treat the evil world in evil ways. They prefer to cheat to get what they want. Most of them even prefer to steal or kill to get what they want, and they think that they are not doing anything wrong. Do they believe that since the world is already corrupt, why not be like the world? The mind of a psychopath is far more complicated than the average of the human mind. Some scientists came up with the idea to somehow control them. Not a hundred percent control, but they found out a way to connect with them. An approach that could make them easier to read and understand. These methods are still experimental and not thoroughly tested on a large scale, but there is a tendency that they would work on a psychopath.

Methods of Psychopathy

1. Convincing them that they do not stand alone.

Even if you are going to try as much as possible to stay away from them, trying to connect with them is the only way to understand them. But when you talk to them, try and keep an open mind for you not to be influenced by their thoughts. Talk to them and assure them that you are there for them. Get them to open up to you even if it means spending more time with them.

2. Assure them that the world is not full of evil.

Psychopaths hate people because they think it is full of evil people and evil things. What role would you play here? You play the role of an adviser, telling them that the world is quite a bit more than they may have conceived. You may choose to give them pictures of beautiful places, cities, beaches and many more. Let them see how beautiful the world is from your perspective. And if you are persistent for a bit, you might get through to them faster and even more efficiently than you would have ever imagined.

3. Teach them the importance of feelings.

A way to help them could be to teach them the importance of feelings and how it could make their lives better. Make them understand that "having feelings do not make you weak but make you even stronger." They should realize that the feelings we have for each other makes us human beings.

4. Teach them that insensitivity solves nothing.

Psychopaths think that being insensitive is a way of getting back at the world, but you must let them know that it's not true. Make them understand that not everyone in the world is evil. There are still good people around, so being insensitive to everyone they see only makes them as evil as the people they call evil. Stand your ground and make them know that you are in charge and that you are only there to help them.

Psychopathy is a personality trait that many

people today have. So, what are the causes of or psychopathy?

No one knows the causes of psychopathy, but research shows that it could be genetic. Meaning that if a parent is a psychopath, the child could tend to become a psychopath as well.

Another leading cause of psychopathy is when children have bad parents. Other causes include:

1. Drug abuse by parents.

If parents have a problem with drugs and they make their child feel neglected, that child may manifest psychopathy. The child feels rejected and not important. People that faced severe issues with their parents tend towards being a psychopath.

2. Parent and child separation.

When a parent and a child get separated from each other, it can take a toll on the child. The separation can be because of a lawsuit; it might also be because of a divorce or even custody rights. People that do not have their parents with them could be psychopaths later in the future. Even when the child is with one parent and misses the other probably because of a restraining order, it could affect them.

3. Child abuse.

People that get abused as children tend towards being psychopaths, especially when they don't have anyone to protect them. Some children even become serial killers, sadists, and many more because of child abuse. Child abuse is probably one of the significant causes of psychopathy because they start hating people from that particular moment of their lives.

Traits of Psychopathy

A psychopath can exhibit specific characteristics. Habits that may help you identify them. But you should know that these traits are so subtle to the extent that it is tough to spot. Some of those traits include:

1. Emotional characteristics of psychopathy.

Emotions are the reason that it is difficult for them to feel remorse or guilt for others. Psychopathic killers can commit murder are not feel any remorse or guilt afterward. Other emotional trait characteristics include:

• Lack of sympathy

• Lack of emotions. (if they have a little bit of them)

• Reckless and irresponsible to their actions.

2. The social trait of psychopathy.

We have already learned that psychopaths are often lying to get out of any situation weather uncomfortable or not. Other social characteristics are:

* Manipulation.
* Smoothness and charm.
* Overambitious.

3. Lifestyle trait of psychopathy.

Psychopathy can show itself in different traits, and lifestyle is one of them. They can make people do what they want at any time. At this point, they possess the power to become parasites. They feed off others. They take the insecurities of people and feed off of it, in a dangerous and sometimes in a criminal way. You might be with a psychopath and not know that he is feeding off you until it's too late.

Other lifestyle characteristics include:

* Careless.
* Uncontrollable.
* Lack of plans.

4. The antisocial trait of psychopathy.

By now, we all know that psychopaths are antisocial, meaning that they don't have a social life; they hate the thought of having a social life. They are mostly themselves doing absolutely anything but socializing. Some of them would rather be at home all day doing nothing than to go to school and make new friends because let us face it; they hate the world and the people in it. They exhibit this particular trait because they feel that they are better off without a social life. And forcing them to socialize will only make it worse. Because when you push them, and they eventually socialize with a few people, they will make those people exactly the way they are. That's if they are not open-minded, that is.

Some other antisocial characteristics include:

* Bad behavior
* Poor tolerance skills.
* Adaptable to any criminal activity.

Is Psychopathy a Mental Illness?

Yes, it is. Psychopathy can be a psychopathic personality disorder. In this case, the advice could be to talk with a specialist to evaluate the situation carefully. Some studies prove that there is only a hypothesis but no actual experimental treatment for the disease. People have it and tend to live with it their whole lives.

In conclusion, psychopathy is a personality that is one of the most feared among the dark triad because it is almost impossible to decipher. The methods and explanations above will help you spot them out in a crowd and probably change their original orientation about life, the world, and the people in the world. The journey is going to be very far from easy, but if you are willing and ready to help, talk to them as much as possible. If you feel that you would get overly manipulated by them, you can get a well-trained psychologist to help you out. Psychopaths are everywhere; you might be living with one right now.

How can a victim be protected and escape?

There are cases in which you must interact with psychopathy people:

such as parents, brothers, family members, or colleagues.

When a specialist diagnoses a psychopath (a diagnosis made up of tests, experiences), the chapter of what to do opens. Here we could discuss a lot about it. Usually, I would like like to understand what kind of psychopathy you are dealing with and the scenario. Of course, the people involved (often not just one person) need help. In clinical experience, the victims were not aware of their partner; they never understood the seriousness of the situation. Not infrequently psychopaths were the parents, the partner of a lifetime, the bosses, colleagues, friends, neighbors. Sometimes we don't know how to treat with them, and we don' t identify them, we usually suffer more or less consciously. What I consider essential, therefore, is to take immediate action. The proximity to these people has often psychologically deformed, if not damaged, the victims.

The Dark Tetrad

According to Delroy Paulhus, psychologists, and researchers, there are four types of self-centered and socially offensive Dark personalities. People that many of us can meet in our daily lives: the Narcissist, the Machiavellian, the nonclinical Psychopath, and The Sadist.

Recently, the "Positive Psychology" movement seems to have taken many steps forward through the study of what makes people happy, courageous, productive, and self-realized.

Delroy Paulhus proposes a series of studies that deepen the dark side of human personality, the so-called Dark Side.

In "Current Directions in Psychological Science," he affirms that his work on the 'dark side' is in contrast with the popular opinion of positive personality traits. From his point of view, dark personalities are charming than bright and happy people.

Paulhus, in his studies, confirms that psychologists often could make a mistake to recognize these types of people. They all share the tendency to have a high score on the test to measure the lack of empathy towards other people.

Most of them are extroverted and social, so they often make a good impression before proceeding to make the lives of those under their 'clutches' miserable.

However, there are essential differences, and these distinctions have important implications for the kind of harm that these people can do to their partners, family, and colleagues. Accordingly, with Paulhus's definitions:

Narcissists are "grandiose self-promoters who continually crave attention."

Machiavellians are "master manipulators." Their score is higher than narcissists in manipulation. They have a natural propensity to be intricate in the white-collar crimes.

Bernard Madoff, one of the most famous stock swindler, reached the leadership of the New York Stock Exchange, to use his dominant position to bilk his investors out of hundreds of millions of dollars. In 2009 the Judge sentenced the maximum sentence of 150 years of prison.

Psychopaths are "arguably the most malevolent." They get the highest score in terms of insensitivity, impulsiveness, manipulation, and grandiosity, becoming 'obscure' across the board. They have often inclined them towards violence when others get in their way.

Charles Manson is the typical situation of a clinical psychopath. Paulhus affirms that there are many people whose psychopathy is low enough to avoid the prison, while however leading to costs for those who get drawn close to them.

For example, in a job interview, they excel over normal people, benefiting from their lack of anxiety regarding the opinion of other people. They have a greater willingness to show their strengths to strangers while playing smoothly and comfortably.

Sadists share the insensitivity, impulsiveness, and manipulativeness trait with the first three types. They add, to the characteristic trait, the enjoyment of cruelty. Accordingly, with Paulhus's theory, sadists may have jobs such as police officers or the military, where they can legitimately harm others. This affirmation doesn't mean that all law enforcement personnel are sadistic, but simply that their score in the test is higher than the average number of everyday sadists.

Paulhus has a punctilious approach to the measurement of personality traits. It is fundamental to understand the difference between dark personalities because you will have different consequences.

For instance, a Machiavellian employee will create different harm than a narcissist or a psychopath.

This way, Paulhus recommends to the employer to make a severe technique and attention during the selection stage.

Although his work on the Dark Triad is well

known, the researcher is even best known for his work to eradicate the prejudices on the personality tests. He distinguishes the different forms of social desirability that can contaminate the answers to those tests. So, people can obtain the same result on the test but for a different reason.

Considering the harm can cause a Dark person, some people would be glad to get the result of those tests on hand before they chose their long-term mates.

"Insanity is doing the same thing over and over again and expecting different results."

– Albert Einstein

Notes:

_____
_____
_____
_____
_____
_____
_____
_____
_____
_____
_____
_____
_____
_____
_____
_____
_____
_____
_____
_____
_____
_____
_____
_____
_____
_____
_____

"Whatever is rejected from the self, appears in the world as an event."

– *Carl Gustav Jung*

Chapter 6: Expression Of Dark Psychology

In every one of us, there is the capacity for all manner of evil. For some, however, this is not merely a latent capacity. These individuals exhibit the various imaginations arising from their dark subconscious and conscious thoughts in varying degrees. For some, it is a little more than petty crimes. But you can also expect some truly terrifying characters.

The Arsonist

This crime involves the deliberate setting of a

fire, especially when it happens due to malevolent intent. Usually, it happens in protest or retribution, and the object that is on fire is public property or private property which does not belong to the arsonist. Often, when arson happens, the first image in people's minds is one of a burning house or building. Arsonists may set other kinds of properties, real or personal, aflame. The list of things that could be set on fire by an arsonist also includes forest fires.

In some cases, the arsonist is careful not to endanger human lives. But there are many instances where there are confirmed human casualties. And this could be a result of negligence on the part of the arsonist, whereby the loss of human life is entirely unintended. Sometimes, the human fatality may be deliberate and, as such, considered murder.

Several motivating factors could lead a person to commit arson. One of which is insurance fraud. The property owners may hope to trick the institution responsible for upholding their insurance policy. Such characters would, intentionally, set their properties on fire and claim that it happened as a result of other causes rather than their direct involvement.

The most common cause of arson gets linked

to the disorder known as pyromania. The urge for fire setting in such individuals is so strong that many prove powerless to it. The bliss after they have committed the arson is usually a rewarding feeling for them. But, whether intentional or the result of a controlling disorder, the result is often the same.

People who are more prone to having pyromania are those who got abused in their childhood. This abuse is especially evident in cases of sexual abuse. There is also a study which indicates that the act of fire-setting (which is considered arson) as a young person is a precursor to schizophrenia later in life. People with depression and those who abuse drugs have an increased probability of becoming arsonists.

Arson can so be committed that, every year, an average of 60,000 cases of intentional fire-setting are reported yearly in countries like the United States of America and England. These fires account for millions and even billions of pounds and dollars in losses. Also, hundreds of people lose their lives to this raging menace yearly, with about a thousand reported casualties.

The Serial Killer

Popularized by fan fiction and crime documentaries, serial killers, are some of the most feared criminals in history. Serial killing is one that involves concurrent murders by an individual within only a few months. There is often a particularly common method, either in the type of victims, the nature of the killing, or the time between each murder. Serial killers are human predators, and they often embody some behavioral and psychological qualities as actual predators of the wild.

The motivation behind serial killing of any kind is not limited to just one. There quite a few reasons why a person would, as they say, snap. These include anger, retribution, the thrill of it, or to get the attention of any or everyone. The serial killer may keep trophies of his or her kill. Usually, they hold strange collections of parts of the whole of their victims. Some other serial killers may engage in sexual relations with their victims before they kill them, during the killing, or with the corpse.

As is often the case, serial killers feel no remorse for their actions and may only regret getting caught. Ted Bundy, a name many have come to associate with the words deranged serial killer. When he got questioned about the numerous lives which have been extinguished by his hands, he said, "I don't feel guilty for anything."

Their drive to kill could be as impulsive as an obsessive-compulsive disorder. The psychological and sexual gratification after a successful kill is no less than those experienced by pyromaniacs. Serial killers get classified as psychopaths. This classification is because of how detached they can be from the suffering of others. They may be unable to experience emotional pain like ordinary, everyday people.

There is a lively debate regarding the nature of the serial killer and if it is rooted in DNA.

It has shown that psychopathic tendencies are related to abnormal brain functions, do to a not accurately interpretation of the information received from the amygdala.

Some of the names which pop up when serial killers get mentioned include Ted Bundy; probably an infamous household name. He would capture his female victims, sexually abuse them, and then kill them before dismembering the corpses. Often, he would even keep the severed head of his victims as a kind of souvenir. He may have murdered well over 30 individuals.

The name Jeffrey Dahmer would probably make most people pause and shiver in fear. He was a serial killer, but the act he got famous for was cannibalism. As far as deranged can be defined, Jeffery Dahmer did many of what one would expect of a psychopath. He would rape, dismember, and then consume the remains of his victims as a meal. He even performed several experiments with his victims, which included attempting to turn them into his slaves by boring holes into their skulls. Although he, very likely, must have killed a lot more than 17 people, he got convicted of only that number of murders.

Pedro Lopez continues to inspire terror in the hearts of many who remember his murdering spree. This terror is because, although he may no longer be a suspect of any recent killings, no one can determine his location. Pedro Lopez, in the time when he was known as the "Monster of the Andes," was a pedophile, rapist, and serial killer. Of the over 300 people he confessed to the killing, the law convicted him of the murder of 110 girls. After spending 18 years in jail for his crimes, Pedro Lopez got released on good behavior.

The serial killer   Albert Fish, sends an

extremely graphic letter to the mother of one of his victims, detailing how the murder was carried out, it becomes clear how twisted the character is. His primary focus was on little children, whom he would rape and eat. While he proudly claimed to have been responsible for the murders of more than a hundred children, he got convicted of only three of them. He was especially crafty at luring the innocent kids who met fate in the fashion of horror movies. After forcefully have sexual intercourse with the children, he would kill and cut them up in pieces to eat.

The Necrophiliac

Necrophilia is used to define sexual intercourse with a dead body. Those who engage in such acts find themselves only attracted to corpses and may not find living human beings to be sexually appealing. But these characteristics do not account for the majority of the reason why specific individuals practice necrophilia, at least not according to Resnick and Rosman. Their study revealed that the need to be in control of a sexual partner who does not reject or struggle with them surpasses every other need. Going by the same study, an attraction to dead bodies only accounts for 15% of the reason why some individuals are necrophiliacs.

Like many other individuals who have committed acts of extreme depravity, many necrophiliacs have decent enough IQs. One would expect that to perpetuate an act so vile; the character must have some mental issues. But the data provided by Rosman and Resnick would beg to disagree. Only 11% of the 122 necrophilia cases studied by them proved to be psychotic. The rest had reasonably high intelligence, although most of them did have personality disorders.

One question which is asked frequently about necrophiliacs is whether the behavior is a mental disorder or not. Professionals in Psychology do not regard it as a mental illness. In fact, as opposed to what the everyday guy might feel about sexual intercourse with a corpse, it is not all that abnormal to psychologists. Some individuals prefer to copulate with cars, dolls, and other inanimate items. As such, necrophilia gets listed as a type of paraphilia. Since the corpse would be unable to give consent, necrophilia cannot be said to be nonconsensual intercourse. It is also for this motivation that some consider the act to be fetishistic.

If you have wondered as to whether necrophilia is something peculiar to the human male species, then you may be right. Although there have been many cases of women participating in necrophilia, men hold a higher percentage of this behavior. In the research by Rosman and Resnick, it showed that, of the candidates chosen for their study, the necrophiliacs who were men made up 95%. Whether this implies that men are more likely to be necrophiliacs is yet to be determined.

Finally, necrophilia is not a modern phenomenon. It goes back to the embalmers of ancient Egypt and, even, way before then. It is only now that we begin to understand, with tiny steps, the pathology behind the act. Still, there is a lot more to learn about the act of paraphilia.

"Manipulation. Domination. Control. These are the three watchwords of violent serial offenders"
– John E. Douglas

Notes:

"For outward show is a wonderful perverter of the reason."

— *Marcus Aurelius*

Chapter 7 : Selfie, Narcissist And Psychopathy

According to recent studies, the continuous use of social media, as well as posting one's selfies, can be indicators of personality characteristics such as narcissism and psychopathy.

Most of us have an internet connection and use Social Media. It is a way to maintain a relationship with others, and there is no problem with using them.

For some, however, social media becomes a real addiction that interferes with their daily lives.

A new study has examined the relationship between social media addiction, narcissism, and self-esteem.

In the examination of 25,000 people, the researchers found that people dependent on social media ended up with higher levels of narcissism and low levels of self-esteem. Addiction on social media, measured through the Bergen Social Media Addiction Scale, allows a connection made to personality traits. Indeed, it shows that this form of dependence gets linked to higher levels of neuroticism, extraversion, and low levels of conscientiousness.

However, this is the first study where has been analyzed the link between narcissism and self-esteem.

The authors explain that social media triggers activities aimed at increasing the Ego, an aspect that both narcissists and people with low self-esteem search. All social media could work as the perfect scenario of a social arena in which all those can feed his Ego, thanks to the feedback that they will receive. Furthermore, the lack of face-to-face interaction can be attractive to those with low self-esteem.

There is nothing wrong with being happy, receiving an appreciation through a "LIKE" or amusing tweets. When you begin to crave that feedback more and more, it may be time to review how addicted you are to the button and how "happiness" is somehow depending on that.

"Selfie" is part of the Oxford online dictionary since 2012. It Means "a photograph that one has taken of oneself, typically with a smartphone or webcam and uploaded to a social media website."

A study published in the journal "Personality and Individual Differences" examined the relationship between posting Selfies, Photo-Editing, and personality.

The question the researchers asked is the following: Do are people posting selfies on social media narcissists, psychopaths, self-objectifying, or both?

The authors studied self-objectification, along with three traits that at this point, all of us will recognize as the "dark triad": narcissism, psychopathy, and Machiavellism.

To examine the association between selfies and personalities, Fox and Rooney used a representative sample of 1000 men between 18 and 40 years old. Participants filled out personality questionnaires that assessed both aspects of the dark triad and self-objectification.

They asked how many selfies they had taken and posted on social media in the last week. As well as how many photos they had published and how much time they spent on social media.

It has also been asked to assess how often they used applications to look better in photos, such as cropping the image, using filters and various touches.

The results showed that both narcissism and self-objectification were associated with higher spending of time on social media than with photo editing.

The publication of numerous selfies was related to both narcissism and psychopathy; Machiavellism was not associated with the behavior of the photo when these other variables get considered.

This study shows that narcissists are more likely to post selfies and make efforts to look better in photos.

It is interesting to note that psychopathic men have published more selfies, but they have not attempted to modify them as narcissistic counterparts.

The authors of the study presumed that this could be because they lack self-control and therefore, do not need to filter or edit their photos.

The study underlines a high perception of

"Ego" that is more evident in a narcissist than a psychopath.

When does a fun photo become an obsession?

If you are continuously picking up your phone and clicking, watch out—you may suffer from selfitis.

The obsessive need to post selfies, defined as 'selfitis' according to a term coined in 2014, is a real mental disorder. Psychologists from Nottingham Trent University and the Thiagarajar School of Management in India that happened to get published in the International Journal of Mental Health and Addiction monitored the phenomenon. They discovered that it not only exists but there are three categories: the chronic one, the acute and borderline.

The 'selfitis' is defined as "chronic" when there is an uncontrollable need to take pictures of themselves, 24 hours a day — posting them on Facebook and Instagram more than six times a day. It is "borderline" if you take selfies at least three times a day, but without necessarily publishing them on social media. While it is classified as "acute" if you make a lot of self-portraits and then all are published online. The Psychologists surveyed 400 people in India, a country that has many Facebook users, and that has the highest deaths related to 'dangerous' selfies.

They create a real 'selfitis scale.' The researcher made a test with 20 statements answering by assigning a score of up to a maximum of 5 to find the category of this disorder (the most serious is the chronic). Inside there are phrases like "I earn a lot of attention by posting selfies on social networks" or "Making selfies improves my mood and makes me feel happy." Not all Researchers, however, agree that the 'selfitis' exists, indeed for some, it is the only 'to give it a name' that makes it real.

Are you enjoying Dark Psychology Secrets? If so, we would be glad to receive a short review on Amazon. It means mean a lot to us. Thank you.

"To be, or not to be - that is the question"
– William Shakespeare

Notes:

_____

_____

_____

_____

_____

_____

_____

_____

_____

_____

_____

_____

_____

_____

_____

_____

_____

_____

_____

_____

_____

_____

_____

_____

_____

_____

_____

"It's easier to fool people than to convince them that they have been fooled."

— *Mark Twain*

Chapter 8: Brainwashing

Are You Brainwashed About Brainwashing?

If you ask someone if they know what brainwashing is, they will probably reply that they do. Brainwashing is a concept that many people have heard of while mistaking their vague familiarity for accurate understanding. Of all the dark psychology techniques contained in this book, brainwashing has the most serious and broadest impact. If the other dark psychology techniques are sniper bullets, aimed at one particular person, brainwashing is a nuclear bomb capable of devastating an entire city.

The term brainwashing refers to the process

of changing a person's thoughts about identity and belief with new ideas that suit the purpose of the person doing the brainwashing. It can occur in both wider and narrower contexts. For example, a brainwasher can control one person in particular, or use the same techniques and principles to control the minds of a whole group. It is the way that makes atheists into suicide bombers and prisoners of war allies of the enemy. It has been tested and proven over the years to be effective in almost any scenario.

So, what are the most common misunderstandings related to brainwashing? Many people picture the process as some quick and forced occurrence. Picture either Alex in "A Clockwork Orange" or Neo in "The Matrix" having concepts forced into their skull, involuntarily, in a short space of time. This brainwashing from Hollywood is far from what occurs in real life.

The process of real-world brainwashing will be explored in detail later in this chapter. The process involves the slow and seemingly spontaneous variation of a person's "map of reality." From the one, they have freely had to one that is forced upon them by the brainwasher. The incredible irony of the technique is the brainwasher will ensure the victim feels in control at all times.

Brainwashing Contexts

So, what are some of the main situations that are fertile breeding grounds for brainwashers? Before the process of brainwashing itself gets explored thoroughly, let's take a look at the cases in which people get brainwashed and the motivations behind this.

A lot of people would agree with the idea that "cults brainwash people," but few would be able to explain what a cult is and how they brainwash their recruits. Let's demystify the process. A cult is a fringe group, often built around a charismatic leader who can exert high levels of influence over their followers. The cult will usually provide a "complete understanding of reality" to those who follow it. Why exactly is this cult context one in which brainwashing flourishes?

The primary attraction of cults is they present reality as something straightforward and within reach of the average person, provided the person is willing to take on board the cult's teachings. We live in a complex modern world where life can seem confusing and overwhelming. Cults cut through this confusion and tell people, "don't worry; we have the answer." How this "answer" gets presented is intended to play on the human need for belonging and acceptance. Brainwashing can flourish in this context as a result of the idea of the "new normal."

What exactly is "the new normal"? It is a way in which cults can influence those they brainwash into accepting their teachings by making them seem prevalent, accepted, and positive. For example, the idea of worshipping a man who claims to be God would be incredibly strange in everyday life. Within the closed environment of a cult, however, this behavior becomes "normal" to the extent that not doing it would seem strange to people within the cult! This process of persistent, social reinforcement is one of the most potent ways in which the ideological brainwashing of cults can occur.

Think of cults as drug dealers. Perhaps the newcomer to the cult had been seeking something in their lives and came across the cult, just as newcomers to the world of drugs often, misguidedly, seek out the first high of their own volition. The cult doesn't need to "push" the drug of their ideology onto the victim as the victim was already seeking the fulfillment of a void in their life. It is this initial "search" and "readiness" on the part of the people who get brainwashed, later on, makes them so susceptible to the brainwashing process itself.

Ideologies are another context, similar to cults, in which brainwashing is commonplace. The main difference between a cult and an ideology is that the focus of the ideology is on the idea itself rather than the person delivering the message and those who follow them. Whereas cults brainwash people into placing faith and trust in the cult leader and their followers, ideological brainwashing involves leading people to put absolute trust in an idea.

Ideological brainwashing is unbelievable dangerous due to the fact it goes above and beyond any one individual. Think of extremist religious terrorism, for example. It is possible for a high profile figure within the ideology, such as Osama Bin Laden, to be killed. Does this kill support for the idea itself? No! The dead figures get praised as martyrs who gave their lives to the ideology, thus increasing its attractiveness and allure to potential newcomers.

Almost any ideology is likely to have an

extremist, fringe outskirt in which brainwashing takes place. Even something seemingly innocent like a pop band can have this impact. Young fans, at a psychologically impressionable age, link their sense of identity, happiness, and belonging to a pop group. They will gladly defend this group to extents that are unusually intense. Some pop groups have fans that even self-harm, using razor blades if a member quits the group! If you carefully consider this phenomenon of the power of brainwashing even in accidental, innocent contexts, then consider how devastating the process can be in intended settings like cults and terrorist groups.

Now that you have a better consciousness of the way brainwashing can occur in broader social contexts, such as cults and ideologies, it is essential to understand that a personal, one-on-one context is also a ripe situation for elements of brainwashing to occur. There are similarities and differences between "group" and "individual" brainwashing and understanding these nuances can help to identify when either type is occurring.

Personal brainwashing is similar to group brainwashing as it involves the slow and steady replacement of existing beliefs with new beliefs that serve the objectives of the brainwasher.

Instead of relying on group dynamics to reinforce "the new normal," a one on one brainwashing situation will instead rely on a deep, personal connection between the brainwasher and the victim. This situation can be even more powerful than group brainwashing as the content can be modified and altered to the particular psychological constitution of the victim.

The Process of Brainwashing

Now that you understand the reality of what brainwashing is, and where it occurs, let's take a look at the specific process itself. Distinctions will show the difference between how the method applies to both group and individual situations.

The starting point of any episode of brainwashing is the mental state and social circumstance of the victim. It is the foundation upon which the process is entirely reliant. Brainwashing is not something that can be carried out on absolutely anyone. It requires the identification of a person who is seeking something or trying to fill a void in their life.

So what kind of people are ideal victims for brainwashers? People who have had their existing reality shaken up by a recent event are prime targets for brainwashers. For example, many of the Western men who have traveled to become terrorists in Syria, and detonate suicide bombs, have done so after the death of a close friend or relative. When their real-world loses its meaning and certainty, brainwashers can step in and provide that certainty in the form of a murderous ideology.

Once a brainwashing victim has been identified, either in person or via the Internet, the actual process of brainwashing begins. Contrary to the popular image of a brainwasher as a wide-eyed psychopath who will incessantly and angrily indoctrinate their victim, real-world brainwashers are anything but this. They will come across as calm, friendly, rational people who have their lives together in a way the victim does not. Imagine being homeless and being befriended by a celebrity. This situation is how the process of meeting their brainwasher for the first time feels for a victim.

The brainwasher will often work initially on creating a level of trust and rapport between themselves and their victims. This scenario usually involves creating both deep and superficial similarities. For example, superficial similarities may suggest surface level preferences like the enjoyment of the same sport or even food! Deeper level rapport may involve some "deep" shared experience in the past of both the brainwasher and the victim. Brainwashers will convincingly fake these if needed. If the victim shares the fact that they have lost a relative in the past, guess what? The brainwasher suddenly has a similar story to tell.

The false emotional warmth and connection explained above is not the only aspect of brainwashing that occurs initially. The brainwasher will often provide gifts and other favors to their victims. For example, the brainwasher may treat them to meals or send them gadgets or other useful items. This scenario creates a sense of gratitude and indebtedness from the victim to their brainwasher and softens up any resistance the victim may initially experience.

One of the most precise patterns of the above initial kindness is from the Prisoner of War camps. When American troops got captured in the past, their captors often offer them American cigarettes and respectfully speak to them. This situation reverses the expectations of the victim and opens the victim's mind to the further brainwashing process that is to follow.

A perfect presentation is a next step in the brainwashing process, following the initial victim identification and rapport building stages. This process involves the brainwasher slowly and increasingly offering a solution to all of the problems that the victim has opened up. This process is always done in a casual, offhand way at first to avoid any negative experiences of pressure the victim may experience otherwise. This utopian solution is still whatever cult, ideology or personality the brainwasher is trying to convert their victim to—terrorism, religious sect or just a charismatic brainwasher's own need for validation and praise.

When performed correctly, the initial stages of this process will leave a victim craving more and more information and understanding of the solution that is a hint of this process happening. The brainwasher may even withhold this information initially as if it is something that the victim must work at being worthy of attaining. This situation will lead to a strong motivation on behalf of the victim to seek out and accept the information they get provided. Thanks to the preceding steps, the poisonous ideas that get implanted into the victim will seem as natural and refreshing as cold water on a hot day.

Once the victim is being spoon-fed snippets of their new belief system and responding well to them, the brainwasher will be very careful to reveal the right things at the right time. This concept is sometimes known as "milk before meat" or "gradual revelation." It involves the presentation of easy to accept ideas before anything controversial gets revealed. For example, in the case of religious terrorism, recruiters may initially focus on convincing their victims that God loves them. This situation is usually quite acceptable. More objectionable ideas, such as God wants you to blow yourself up, are saved until far further down the line. At this point, the brainwashing has reached the point of no return.

You may be questioning why a victim continues to engage with their brainwasher once the objectionable ideas begin to become apparent. The reason is threefold. First, the already vulnerable victim now feels a strong sense of liking and approval of their brainwasher.

Second, the victim has invested time and sometimes money into the process thus far. This scenario is called the "sunk cost fallacy." The victim is unwilling to "throw away all their hard work" by walking away from the process.

Finally, the brainwasher is likely to have amassed a lot of secretive and sensitive information on their victim. This "dirt" can then be held over the victim's head, either discreetly or overtly.

Both the ideas of a vulnerable victim and the "sunk cost fallacy" make logical sense. The concept of blackmail and control may be harder to understand at first. Why would a victim respond well to such threats? Well, they usually do not get presented in a threatening way. For example, if the victim has divulged a lot of sensitive information to a brainwasher, and then begins to give signs of walking away, the brainwasher may appear concerned and insist that "if I can't help you any more with your problems, I need to make sure someone else can. Perhaps your family or boss needs to know what's been going on with you, so they can look out for you when I'm not there."

Because of the deep sense of rapport and warmth, the brainwasher has manipulated their victim into feeling, the above form of blackmail and control is often actually perceived as kind, compassionate behavior. It is usually enough to make the victim see "sense" and agree to remain on the brainwashing path they have embarked.

Brainwashers are adept at making the pain and struggle of walking away seem epic, so staying becomes the preferable, easy option by default.

The end product of this process is the victim believing everything they have been indoctrinated to view as the truth. The power of the process is that the victim will feel they have chosen these views as their own and have sought them out through their own volition. This process leaves a previously normal individual as an indoctrinated psychological slave to something they have no idea even exists.

The Impact of Brainwashing

The above analysis of the brainwashing process shows the severity and depth of the technique. It is inevitable that a process as powerful as this has lasting consequences. Some of the main impacts of brainwashing after the process that gets completed will now get explained.

Loss of identity is one of the most severe side effects of brainwashing. A feature of many cults and ideologies is that people who complete their initiation process get a new name. This situation allows the person's psyche to detach from their old identity. They can believe things and do things they would never have done before as the person they used to be no longer exists. When carried out carefully, the brainwashing process leaves a victim feeling as if their old identity was no more real or permanent than a nightmare from which they have awoken.

So is brainwashing merely a process of ideas? Not at all. If brainwashing resulted in only the change of opinions, then it would be far less of a problem than it is. The main danger of brainwashing is it changes not only the ways that people think and feel but also the way they behave. People go from functional members of the society with acceptable, positive jobs and interests to brainwashed zombies willing to carry out rape, murder, and suicide. This situation sounds sensational and dramatic, but it's true. Read on for the proof.

If you have any doubts about what brainwashing can drive a person to, consider the following examples. Members of some religious cults will gladly cut off all contact from their family, leave their careers behind, surrender all their wealth and possessions, and place their autonomy entirely in the hands of the organization that has brainwashed them. Also, the victim will see their new lifestyle as a blessing they are fortunate to have, rather than something unpleasant they have get forced to do.

Another example of the toxic outcome of brainwashing is the repeated tale of young people becoming brainwashed by religious extremists to travel to a foreign land and drive a car packed full of explosives into a group of people they have never met and who have never hurt them. Such young victims are often educated people with a track record of success in life and a family history free of turmoil or abuse. These tragic losses of life are a testament to the overwhelming, all-conquering power of the brainwashing process.

PTSD (post-traumatic stress disorder) is another hallmark of those who manage to escape, or are rescued from, a situation of intense brainwashing. Brainwashing victims often show the same physical and psychological signs as war veterans who have witnessed their friends being blown apart next to them during combat. The severity of this traumatic aftermath shows that a brainwashing situation can harm a person as much as a world war.

Perhaps the most shocking examples of the

long-term impact of brainwashing are the numerous instances of people who have to liberate, rescued or escaped from a brainwashing situation, only to later return of their own free will. Even once they are outside of the controlling, brainwashing environment, the legacy of the process runs so deep through a person's mind; they seek to return to it. This situation is a form of Stockholm syndrome. The escapees will praise their brainwashers far into the future and defend, support, and justify the ideological stances they were indoctrinated with while captive.

"I will not let anyone walk through my mind with their dirty feet."

– Mahatma Gandhi

Notes:

_____
_____
_____
_____
_____
_____
_____
_____
_____
_____
_____
_____
_____
_____
_____
_____
_____
_____
_____
_____
_____
_____
_____
_____
_____

"Whoever controls the media, controls
the mind"

— *Jim Morrison*

Chapter 9: Subliminal Messages

The word subliminal takes root from the Latin SUB and LIMEN, literally translated into below the threshold.

It refers to the boundary between the conscious and the subconscious.

The subliminal message must reach the subject to which it is destined to an unconscious level, thus ending up subconsciously perceived.

Subliminal messages can end up sent in many ways, through images, sounds, written texts, and music. It illustrates a specific topic, but which sends a sort of code into the memory of the victim. It hides a different meaning from the main context.

The compelling aspect of subliminal messages is that you can say one thing to a person, and he will understand something different. While this conscious mind digests something that they are willingly approving, their subconscious mind may be hearing something completely different. Because you have put them right into a responsive mode, they are more likely to respond in the manner you want. Even their subconscious mind is much more ready to approve the information.

You are programming their mind with your desired messages, and they have no suggestion that you are doing so.

Mind control is a useful technique that can help you to have people thinking as you want. Due to this masterful ability to control their minds without them also recognizing it, you will have the skill to have any result easily.

The first to use subliminal messages was the advertising agent James Vicari. Thanks to the tachistoscope, an equipment capable of projecting any word on a cinema screen every 5 seconds, for only 1 / 3000th of a second, in a movie theater increased the consumption of drinks and food by 40% in a few weeks by bombarding viewers with messages like: "are you hungry? Eat popcorn," and "Are you thirsty? Drink Coca Cola".

The primary purpose of subliminal messages at the beginning, putting them in films, in background music in supermarkets or bars, was to increase sales of some products.

Many experts argued that there was nothing wrong with suggesting to people what to buy — another way like any other to make the economy run.

In 1978, Dr. Hal Becker, a researcher in electronic medicine, created a machine, the Little Black Box, which got used in the field of theft control. The little black box was designed to spread, in the background music in 37 sample supermarkets, messages like "it's wrong to steal ... I don't steal, don't steal ...".

When the Time publicized this hidden way of dissuading people from stealing, a large group of people did not look favorably on this way. They defined it as a severe violation of freedom of choice.

Becker defended himself by simply saying: "Someday there will be audio conditioning in the same way we now have air conditioning."

The most widespread system, even today, to send subliminal messages is the video system.

They inserted frames during the screening of a movie. Usually, the occult images are sexual or ideological.

Sometimes it happens that what you are watching contains "a movie in a movie."

On January 8, 1999, Disney announced the withdrawal from the market of the Home Video version of the 1977 cartoon The Rescuers, because it would contain a reprehensible image that passes on the background.

In fact, after about 38 minutes from the beginning of the cartoon, the two cute rodents glide among the skyscrapers in the sardine box laced to the back of the Orville gull. In two non-consecutive frames in one of the windows, appears the photo of a topless woman.

Even in Mickey Mouse, we could find subliminal messages.

A symbol appears in the n ° 2412, dated February 19, 2002. Yes, it's a Square, a Compass. It is true that in the adventure, we talk about navigation, and these two tools are used to trace the routes. Here they appear to be crossed precisely in the typical Masonic style.

Another type of "subliminal technique" is the musical one or hidden messages that are found in the songs.

Inside many songs, you can find messages with a commercial, advertising background but also, and above all, messages that instigate drugs, Satanism, sexual depravity, pornography, suicide, and murder.

Author Europe, LP The Final Countdown: «In every time, in every season/ God knows I've tried/ So please don't ask for more/Can't you see it in my eyes/ This might be our last goodbye/ Carrie, Carrie...»;
Backmasking: «He'll rescue, he'll rescue. I could die, god Satan, but I've to play naked in this night. Yes, I got you first. I was surprised one night. I say you a secret thing. »

Author Prince, LP Purple Rain; Darling Nikki.
Backmasking: «Hello! How are you? I'm fine, 'cause I know that the Lord is coming soon. Coming, coming soon. Ah-ah-ah-ah-ah...»

Author Queen, LP   A Kind of Magic; One Vision
Backmasking: «Oh, my sweet Satan, I've seen sabbà.»

Even if the technique of listening to a reverse track, with which these messages get discovered, is not considered reliable, it could anyway affect our mind.

What is the consequence of subliminal messages?

The subliminal message is a sort of whisper that we perceive on a sensory level. We lurk in our subconsciously reveals itself to our conscious in the form of desire.

"Are you hungry? Eat popcorn, Are you thirsty? Drink Coca Cola"

We don't feel forced to buy popcorn or Coca Cola; we only feel the need.

Let's reflect on the many taboos that in the last few decades have fallen, leading to the limelight of sexual perversions. An increase of satanic cult to torture and murder could also be consequences of the occult and unconscious manipulation? Especially on those subjects who are psychologically fragile and easily manipulated, who are not able to discern their desires from those induced.

Being victims for many years of all sorts of this unconscious and shameless manipulation, do we know how to distingue the real needs from the one induced?

Some psychiatrists claim that these messages, if heard frequently and in particular situations, under the influence of drugs or alcohol, prey to moments of depression, in a specific difficult period, can negatively influence the behavior by creating states of hallucination, raptus, aggression, up to lead, at times, to suicide or murder.

Is it possible to defend ourselves from this type of message? And how can it be done even for the most unconscious ones?

The answer comes from a recent study offered by Johan C. Karremansa and colleagues from the University of Amsterdam. The researcher informed a group of people that they were going to receive subliminal messages. The pure awareness had the function of a protective shield.

Even if they distract increasing the degree of unconscious perception with another exercise like an anagram, the result was the same. The subjects who know they are going to receive a subliminal message, even if very distracted and busy (in the anagrams) can prevent the persuasive effect of the message.

Here are four tricks that I think can facilitate this "self-defense" process:

1) Be aware of your needs: If you are in the supermarket and with an empty stomach, likely, you will end up influenced by advertising and

product packaging. In this context, you have two options: eat before you go or keep this in mind.

2) Study: know the levers of persuasion and manipulation. From NLP (Neuro-Linguistic Programming) techniques, you'll find a lot of precious methods to understand and manage the most subtle manipulation techniques. NLP techniques are in use both in businesses and personal relationships to affect people around you. NLP techniques help you get your message across in the correct way so that they are interpreted by the people to give you your desired outcomes. NLP also focuses on the right use of language to help you motivate people around you to get something useful done.

3) Study the language: most of these messages go through the word, from the salesman who speaks to you in a certain way to the written message. A right way is to learn the linguistic models of NLP;

4) work on yourself: increase your awareness by meditating or discovering your values and your goals. In short, work on yourself to get to know yourself more deeply. Knowing ourselves is the starting point to avoid this type of message. Be aware of what you want, and what you don't want is one of the most potent mental positions ever.

It is good to know in advance if a message contains subliminal suggestions, but it is impossible to know for sure and to anticipate it in every context. Therefore, I think it is useful to study and work on yourself.

It is fascinating to note that the right information could have an "anti-virus" effect that can sabotage the impact of subliminal messages.

The study shows you the principles of persuasion and works on yourself that allows you to have that clarity of anti-persuasion intent typical of the shopping list. If you go shopping without a detailed list, you will most likely become influenced by the advertisements around you. The absence of clarity, we cling to the first glimmer of solidity.

The monster from which we must defend ourselves is ignorance and the lack of precise information. And it still shows us how fundamental awareness is of ourselves and our surroundings.

"These subliminal aspects of everything that happens to us may seem to play very little part in our daily lives. But they are the almost invisible roots of our conscious thoughts"

– *Carl G. Jung*

Notes:

"The most painful thing is losing yourself in the process of loving someone too much, and forgetting that you are special too."

— *Ernest Hemingway*

Chapter 10 : Manipulation In Relationships

Emotional manipulation or being in a manipulative relationship is one of the most unfortunate things a person can experience. Not only does it destroy your sense of self-worth, but it also prevents you from enjoying fulfilling and rewarding relationships in the future. Manipulation goes against the ethos of a healthy, happy, positive, and inspiring relationship.

While we are all in some way or the other manipulating our loved ones, it becomes sinister when it hits a person's emotions or sense of self-worth for fulfilling a selfish agenda. Here are some effective deals for dealing with manipulation in relationships.

1. Carefully observe your feelings after every interaction. Do most of your conversations or interactions with your partner make you feel

confused, unworthy, or overcome by self-doubt? By doing a routine check of your feelings, you will be able to identify a clear cause.

"It is beyond my control"
— *Vicomte De Valmont*

For example, if you realize that you always feel guilty after a conversation with your partner. Rewind to the discussion and go over what your partner said after each interaction. How did it start? What are the common words and phrases they use while talking to you? Is there a pattern to what they say and how they make you feel?

Please make a note of your feelings to identify the emerging pattern quickly.

Tell yourself that the problem is them and not you. Remember that you are only getting hoodwinked into thinking it is your fault or you aren't good enough. The manipulator is most likely dealing with grave issues of their own, which they are incapable of handling effectively. This instance is only to help you establish a context for their acts, not to make you feel sympathetic towards them. Keep in mind, manipulators seldom deserve sympathy!

2. Assess your relationship objectively. If you can't determine if you are genuinely in a manipulative relationship or the person, get a reality check by talking to friends or people you trust.

Ask them for an objective assessment of your relationship frankly. Do you think your partner has unreasonable expectations from you? Do you think your partner is taking advantage of you? Do you are emotionally vulnerable?

Sometimes by talking to a third person, we gain a perspective we hadn't considered before. It'll probably give you a new way of looking at things, which will allow you to act if you end up getting manipulated.

3. Confront the manipulator. Consider various angles before going for the kill and confronting your manipulator. They most likely won't admit to their manipulative acts, especially if you sound unsure and nervous.

Rather than making blanket statements about how "they have been using you" or "taking advantage of you," get down to specifics. How does a specific action or words make you feel? List instances where you thought you got used. Follow this up with a positive and gentle yet assertive request to mend their behavior.

You are communicating with the manipulator that you are aware of their tricks, which makes them more cautious while manipulating you. In the same vein, you are also allowing them to get their act together. It will take real effort and commitment on your part to move out of an emotionally manipulative relationship. You will have to stay vigilant and develop limitless reserves of self-esteem and positivity.

4. Hit hard at the center of their gravity. If nothing else seems to work, it struck the manipulator on his/her center of gravity. They'll often resort to evil strategies such as befriending your friends and then speaking evil about you or tempting you with a reward and then backing off or not honoring their commitment.

Since you know the person inside out, hit them where it hurts the most. Their center maybe their friends, followers, or anything they think is integral to their existence. Use this knowledge to beat them in their own game.

5. Don't fit in with their ideas. The key to avoid being manipulated is to reinvent yourself and have your thoughts about things rather than subscribing to theirs. Manipulators will shove their beliefs down your throat since they need to control you to further their agenda. Have your

unobstructed views, ideas, and opinions about various aspects of your life. Consistently drilling a design in your mind is how they can successfully confine you in a box.

Don't try to fit in; focus on reinvention. Work hard towards standing out from the rest. Be different, unique, and remarkable in your way. Personal growth and building your self-esteem are the key to fighting manipulation.

6. Don't compromise. Guilt is a powerful emotion leveraged by manipulators. They will use your self-doubt and guilt to their advantage. The agenda is to knock your sense of balance and instill a sense of uncertainty with you. This uncertainty eventually drives you to compromise on your values, ideals, and goals.

Avoid feeling guilty or compromising. Don't doubt yourself or your abilities. Even though you are in a relationship with a person, you don't owe them anything if you do not get treated with respect. Every person deserves to feel beautiful and positive about themselves. If a person doesn't make you feel good about yourself or your accomplishments, there may be a problem. Have a firm belief in your values and ideals. Don't compromise on your values, beliefs, goals, and ideals. Remember, you deserve to feel great about yourself and your achievements. There should be a strong sense of self-belief, self-assuredness, and confidence in what you are doing.

A manipulator becomes powerless in the face of high self-confidence. They start losing their influence once you learn to operate with confidence and refuse to compromise on anything that undermines your self-respect or core values.

7. Don't seek permission. Doing so is like handing the manipulator the pass to manipulate you as they wish. The trouble is, since childhood, we've been conditioned to seek permission. As an infant, we ask permission to eat and sleep. All through school, we are requesting permission to visit the bathroom, eat our lunch, or drink water.

A direct consequence of this is, even as grown-ups, we don't stop seeking permission from people close to us. Instead of informing your partner you are planning to meet a friend over lunch, you'll subconsciously ask them if it is alright if you plan something with your friend. By continuously and habitually seeking permission, you are only giving control of your life to someone else, especially if he/she is a more manipulative type.

"The meeting of two personalities is like the contact of two chemical substances: if there is any reaction, both are transformed."

— *Carl Gustav Jung*

Don't be overly concerned about being polite or making others feel good at the cost of your comfort and happiness. Remember, you have the right to live your life exactly the way you want to. Emotional manipulation is about making you feel indebted or enslaved by some imaginary rule that exists only in the mind of the manipulator. They'll never want you to feel self-sufficient and take your own decisions because that diminishes their hold over you.

There's no need to bow to their authoritative dictates or consult them before everything you do unless it does impact them in a meaningful manner. I happened to have a co-worker who would seek his girlfriend's permission even before going for a coffee break or out for lunch. It was ridiculous the way she treated him and tried to control every move of his. Predictably, the relationship ended on a sour note.

However, no one can make you feel miserable without your permission. And by continually seeking approval, you are giving your partner permission to make you feel unhappy – if that makes sense. You can disregard the manipulator's obsession with confining you anytime by living your life the way you to, without their interference or permission.

8. Be open to new opportunities. The manipulator wants you to put all your eggs in their basket so they can throw away the basket whenever they fancy. Don't lock yourself into them or be tied down by a commitment you aren't comfortable making. Don't be content or accept your current life. If you are in a highly manipulative or emotionally/physically abusive relationship, attempt to break free and explore other relationships or opportunities.

Manipulators in relationships often take advantage of the fact that their partner is "used to them," "addicted to them," "can't do without them" or "can't get anyone better." We often stay in abusive relationships because we believe that we don't deserve any better or won't get anyone better. There is a fear of loneliness or a false sense of being in the cocoon of a relationship.

Break free from such self-limiting and unhealthy thought patterns. Of course, you deserve better in life or will find someone who treats you with respect and dignity. To keep you in your place, manipulators will resort to plenty of name-callings. If you express a desire, they will make you feel like you are arrogant, selfish, proud, cold, and inhumane and many other uncharitable labels.

They want to keep you being codependent on them. By seeking out new opportunities for jobs, relationships, hobbies, etc., you are only weakening their control over you. Seek out new people, make new friends, join a hobby club, a volunteer with an NGO. Do something purposeful and meaningful that allows you to meet new people and live a more intentional life. Doing so is the only way to start becoming self-sufficient and independent.

9. Don't be a baby. If you get fooled once or twice, you are vulnerable, but if you continuously let people walk over you without learning your lessons, you are a downright idiot. Stop letting manipulators take advantage of your gullibility. Develop self-awareness about manipulators and know how they operate. Have enough self-respect to refuse manipulators.

I know a lot of people who sleepwalk through life, allow people to take advantage of them and then blame others for their situation. You can't go around oblivious to manipulators trying to use you to fulfill their agenda. Rather than blaming the evil around you, become smart and take control of your life. Yes, the unfortunate truth about life is cynical and manipulative people exist. The take advantage of people to further their agenda

However, this shouldn't be your ticket to making the same mistakes again and again and crying foul. Manipulators cannot manipulate without the permission of their victims. Accept responsibility for your success and failure. If you are outsmarted or out strategized, it isn't someone else's fault. Learn from past mistakes. Watch out for a pattern that may reveal your vulnerabilities. Don't keep trusting the wrong people again and again.

Similarly, don't keep giving a chronically manipulative person multiple chances. Break free from them. Remove manipulators from your life. Commit to the pursuit of surrounding yourself with positive, encouraging, and like-minded folks who don't take advantage of you.

Remember, you have total control over your life. Place your bets on yourself and not on other people. If you place your bets on other people or rely excessively on other people for your happiness, you make yourself more vulnerable to manipulation.

Again, manipulation victims are not very confident about their judgments. Learn to trust your decisions and instincts. You know what is right for you are much better than anyone else. Don't go around asking people things such as "What am I good at?", "what I do," "who is the real me" etc. You are merely opening the doors of manipulation. Don't go around demonstrating your lack of understanding about yourself.

Again, I know a lot of people who go around seeking constant validation from others. They look at other people to define them. These people won't even buy a pair of trousers if others don't approve of it. Why should others describe you?

Define yourself and trust your judgment. Winners are not people who have a more evolved ability to listen to others. They are the ones who have developed the ability to tune in to their beliefs and judgments. They don't rely on external validation or approval of their ideas. An established trust in your opinions and judgments makes manipulators powerless. When you don't seek validation from others, they don't have an upper hand of how they make you think and feel. Start trusting your instinct and judgment!

10. Dependent manipulators. This situation is a little opposed to the stereotypical image of a manipulator, but they exist. Contrary to most manipulators, a dependent manipulator will continuously make you feel like they are powerless and utterly dependent on you. They accord you a higher position in a relationship to such as extent that you feel emotionally exhausted while dealing with them.

The way to handle this type of manipulation is to get them to make decisions gradually. Make them realize that they are as much responsible for their well-being as you are. They consciously put them into positions where they are forced to decide. Talk to them about how their lack of responsibility to decision making is stressful for you. Over time, they may enjoy taking responsibility.

"And we all know love is a glass which makes even a monster appear fascinating"
— *Alberto Moravia*

Notes:

_____
_____
_____
_____
_____
_____
_____
_____
_____
_____
_____
_____
_____
_____
_____
_____
_____
_____
_____
_____
_____
_____
_____
_____
_____
_____
_____

"Manipulation, fueled with good intent, can be a blessing. But when used wickedly, it is the beginning of a magician's karmic calamity."

– *T.F. Hodge*

Chapter 11: Psychopathic At The Workplace

Usually, we can choose our partner, friends, our gym mate. Rarely we can select our colleague. In this chapter, we will treat only nonclinical cases.

From this book, we learned how to recognize a psychopathic, and we understood that it is challenging, and even dangerous, to get in touch with them.

It is appropriate to make two categories to better understand with which kind of psychopathic colleagues we are working every day and how to deal with them.

The harmless psychopathic colleague

They probably don't have a social life outside of work, or you never want to be among his friends. Your colleague lives in "his world." He doesn't seem to cultivate any hobbies, he greets with difficulty, and he will never be the one to start the conversation. Maybe he is shy, or he has some social phobia.

What can we do?

Try to be kind to him/her.

Regards as first in the morning! Maybe he will not notice your kindness but could help him to see that the world is not so dangerous.

Move as first

There is a new project, and you must work closely with him. The boss asks you for ideas and proposals and expects you to find them together. The mere fact of having to 'start' as first, could make him in the panic. So, be patient and propose yourself. Certainly, when the project gets started, it will be easier for him to proceed and, perhaps, he might surprise you with some excellent ideas.

Try to guide him out of his comfort zone

Follow this advice only if you care about this person. When you seem to have won his trust, try to propose something different. Maybe you can invite him to have a coffee break, or you can bring him a croissant from a coffee shop, or you can tell him about the last beautiful movie you saw on TV.

If you decide to try this route, remember that you always must have a 'Plan B.'

For instance, if you invite him to have coffee, make sure there aren't ten other people with you. You would intimidate him even more, and you would only get a rejection even for the next time. Or if you realize that when you talk to him about that beautiful movie you've seen, he will not participate in the conversation, don't worry. Go back to doing your job. You gave him a chance and he, even if he didn't show you, could have noticed and appreciated it.

Don't have expectations

Not having expectations could be the most crucial advice. If your colleague has this attitude, there will be reasons, and you are certainly not the person who can and must solve this issue. So, don't expect significant changes or miracles. Maybe he will never be the soul of the party, or you will never go for a drink together after work. But you can live with it very well. Remember: you did not choose him as a life partner; he is just a work colleague.

The harmful 'psychopathic' colleague

The second category is much more laborious to deal with; these are the "strange" or "difficult" colleagues that can make your life and your colleague's life very difficult.

They can pollute the whole environment around them, and it is not easy to manage them.

This situation shows you how a psychopathic colleague can behave:

He is addicted to gossip
With you, he talks badly about the other colleagues' and, you can be sure, he does the same with them towards you.

He always complains
Nothing goes well: the cleaning of the office, the position of the desk, the schedules, the organization, the hierarchy. Although the management of the company has changed several

times, and everything has become revolutionized in a thousand different ways, nothing was wrong with him before, and nothing is ok now either.

He always wants to be right

During the meetings, he does not even listen to what the others are proposing. He has only the purpose of being the winner. He is pathologically competitive; he is happy when he will reach his goal, or he has decided to be the best for everyone. The outcome of these battles also depends on his position in the company. The higher it is, the easier it is to get what he wants. But even if it were not so, do not fool yourself. He is the one who, the next time, will be more aggressive than before to defend his questionable opinions.

He's a liar

It certainly cannot be said that he has no imagination. He will change innumerable times his version to avoid admitting the error. The problem is that sometimes even he no longer remembers them and ends up telling different stories to the whole office. But, be careful, if you try to expose him in front of the boss, it could become worse and, to defend his reputation. He will be disposed to take any action to make you pay the cost.

Manipulator

He usually chooses some people he considers sweet, kind, courteous, and helpful and tries to exploit them for his power games. To be the best, he always tries to create adepts to support him. With these unfortunate people, the psychopathic colleague plays a double game. When he finds himself face to face with them, he will be complacent and falsely tries to take them to his side, making them feel important. However, as soon as the opportunity comes, in a meeting or a group, in front of others, he will use them making himself beautiful. In front of everyone, to stand out, his immense Ego will denigrate his victims. Meanwhile, in private, he returns to being kind and fake to continue his dangerous plan.

People that end up chosen for this deceptive game tend to stay disoriented. In most cases, they are sincere, honest, and morally honest people who cannot understand how similar individuals can exist.

"Dividi et Impera."

It has been attributed to Philip II of Macedon

and utilized by the Roman ruler Julius Caesar and the French emperor Napoleon. Literally

means "Divide and Rule." It is a well-known technique for psychopathic and narcissist people. A primary strategy used to assert control is to create divisions among individuals. This technique weakens and segregates them, making it easier to manipulate and dominate. Some are favored, others end up scapegoated. Such dynamics play out very well in a workplace setting.

How to deal with a 'psychopathic' colleague

And here are some tips to manage your colleague and live peacefully in the workplace and even outside.

1. Try to isolate it

Even if you're dealing with a tough psychopath, nobody can live alone. Not even the psychopath is an exception. To carry out his little games, he needs an audience to follow him, to appreciate him or also to be a spectator for his feats.

Don't let him get you involved in situations you don't like or feel uncomfortable with, and when you can, move physically from where he is.

If there is someone with whom you have confidence, invite him to do the same. Leave the psychopathic colleague alone and will he will not be able to carry on his farce for long. Or, in case he continues, his 'circle of negative influence" will be significantly reduced.

2. Speak only about work

Don't let your psychopathic colleague know too much about you. He could also use them negatively against you. Talk to him only when it is necessary and when it is required for your job. If you're talking to some of your colleagues and friends about personal information, don't hesitate to change the subject if he comes. You are not rude. You're just protecting yourself.

3. Take breaks

Sometimes, maybe even often, you must deal with him, and you can't go. In those cases, respect the two previous rules and, after interacting with your psychopathic colleague, remember to take a break. Detoxify yourself from the negativity of that person.

Leave the room, go to the bathroom, go to drink a glass of water or, even better, take two steps out of the building or onto the terrace. If you really can't do any of this (but you can take a break from time to time, right?), Focus on the breath. Take at least three conscious breaths. Make the exhalation longer than inspiration (this stimulates the immediate relaxation) and then calmly resume your activities.

What if the 'psychopath' was your boss?

At your workplace, you could deal with not only a psychopathic colleague, but even with a psychopathic boss!

How to solve the problem? First, apply the suggestions related to your colleagues, you read above also with your boss. If you isolate him, talk about work and try to relax and 'refocus' after each meeting with him you will surely benefit from it.

If, however, the situation is complicated and your life seems like hell, you can consider talking about it with someone.

Even within your workplace, there is probably a human resources office where qualified people work to maintain a peaceful and productive atmosphere in the company.

It is your right to talk to them and explain the situation.

In case you don't have this office, choose a trustable colleague, better if, with higher seniority than yours, to tells about what is happening. Often, we do not confide your secrets because we fear getting judged, but we could find much more understanding than we believe.

A tip: Never talk in 'personal' terms. Try to keep the description of the facts in the workplace. You talk to these people because you can't do your job anymore as you want. Start from here. You will look more professional, and everyone will be more willing to listen to you.

Never fear to ask for help when you need it. It is your right, and you do it for your easiness.

There is interesting research coming from the University of Bonn, entitled "The Role of Interpersonal Influence in Counterbalancing Psychopathic Personality Trait Facets at Work," published in "Journal of Management." The researchers asked a group of 161 people to answer a series of helpful questions to understand their personality, social skills, and work performance. They were asked to evaluate the work behavior of a colleague. The collected data showed that the participants who were part of primary psychopathy and who had social skills were considered collaborative, helpful, kind, and pleasant by their colleagues. On the other hand, the participants who fell into secondary psychopathy were seen by colleagues as destructive, not helpful, and scarce in terms of performance, regardless of social skills.

Conclusion

Not all the people whose personalities have the same traits of psychopathy show antisocial behavior. Indeed, in some cases, they can be excellent work colleagues.

Top 10 Jobs For Psychopaths

Are there professions that make psychopaths? The answer is probably not, although experts believe that there are some trades that more than others attract these kinds of people.

According to the famous text of modern psychology, "Diagnostic and Statistical Manual of Mental Disorders," a psychopathic personality has an exaggerated and grandiose sense of self and is talented in manipulating others.

The psychologist Kevin Dutton's in "The

Wisdom of Psychopaths," takes a surprisingly open-minded technique to the roles that psychos can play in contemporary culture. His checklist looks more a recommendation for a job-hunting psychopath than a cautioning to non-psychopaths about the cunning minds in their midst. The Harvard psychology professor Joshua Buckholtz says, "They're not aliens, they're people who make bad decisions." Let's make a tour on Dutton's Top 10 Jobs for Psychopaths:

10 Civil servants

Jobs that need emotional detachment are excellent for psychotics.

Recently, the UK's Home Office recommended that federal governments to be recruiting psychopaths as a result of their capacity to keep one's cool in an emergency.

9 Chef

The absolute power is intoxicating, even if it's constrained to a separate kitchen area. Psychopaths naturally gravitate toward high-power work.

Usually, they get the best results where others failed. They could efficiently work in a chaotic place, and the kitchen could become the kingdom of chaos, even if it's constrained to a separate kitchen area.

8 Clergy

It might look like one of the most astonishing cases on the list,

The religious organization may legitimate the psychopathic need to manipulate other people. According to Joe Navarro in Psychology today, some people are attracted by professions to manipulate others officially.

7 Police officer

Psychopath, they can keep calm even under stress. Excellent quality for all any other cop. Psychotics grow in unforeseeable situations as well as also do much better when they can make the most of socially approved power dynamics. It's easy to understand why coming to be a police officer would undoubtedly be interesting in the psychopathic mind.

6 Journalist

Concentration, ruthlessness, accuracy, decision, and awareness are beneficial skills to work under pressure and with a short delivery time and to get information from the source that doesn't want to talk.

They will be appropriate to write down stories no matter what the risk will be.

5 Surgeon

They have a short time to make essential and vital decisions. It requires a great ability to manage pressure. It looks like the best job for a psychopath.

One research released in The Bulletin of the Royal College of Surgeons of the UK found that specialists at the health center got a higher rate on the psychopath scale more than the basic population. Teachers in the health centers placed higher on the psychopathy range than those at general hospitals.

4 Salesperson

To make sales needs a higher level of trust in oneself, desire to defeat the competition, and earn more and more. Self-promotion, as well as thoroughly curated representations of reality, can give you amazing results. Not surprising that so many psychos come to be salesmen and saleswomen.

3 Media personality

Most of the presenters, radio, and television have narcissist traits, and for this reason, they may love the popularity and fame. Psychopathy and narcissist commonly go hand in hand, so a place that puts a psycho in front of as many eyes will undoubtedly make them feel very comfortable certainly.

2 Lawyer

Skills like coldness, self-confidence and charm coldness, self-confidence, and charm in the right context can make a good lawyer.

M.E. Thomas, in "Confessions of a Sociopath," talks about how the lack of empathy gives the attorney a great benefit. Convince a jury needs confidence and critical control, all mean of the art of manipulation.

1 CEO

Psychopaths all have what we call "resilience to chaos." Not only they can manage the stress, but they are even better at making stress to create the opportunity to emerge better.

Psychopaths have a strong tendency and opportunity to become corporate leaders, just for their single-minded nature.

This situation, for sure, will not work for all the CEOs.

The psychopath at work and in business cases shows others a deceptive face. The superficial charm looks like charisma and leadership. The grandiose projects represented the expression of a high self-attention; the manipulative attitudes present a manifestation of his persuasion skills.

An interesting article from the FBI suggests which guidelines should end up followed in the investigative stage with psychopathic subjects. Psychopathy has a personality structure in which the inability to feel guilt. The systematic tendency to override and to manipulate others, as well as the construction of a false and unrealistic image himself tends to get used in interpersonal contexts end up prevailing.

Psychopathic has a different mask for each context in which he acts. Sometimes for every single relationship of work or friendship, he enters the mental states of the interlocutor managing to identify the vulnerabilities to exploit them to his advantage.

Similarly, its impulsiveness and the search for risk are a demonstration of energy, capacity for action, ability to perform complex tasks. The unrealistic nature of the objectives that it sets itself is easily confused with a visionary talent. Finally, the lack of empathy could end up recognized as a sign of a predisposition to guide operations with cold blood and strategic planning.

When a psychopathic subject deals with the police, the risks for the investigators are multiple. The fascination with which the psychopath managed to manipulate his collaborators could create a relationship with the investigators, on which he tries to establish the same psychological domination that he sustained in the previous crime.

Usually, he isolates the victims, just like a predator. The investigator needs to make teamwork and cooperation, sharing the information to avoid falling into the trap.

"We are all apprentices in a craft where no one ever becomes a master."

— Ernest Hemingway

Notes:

_____
_____
_____
_____
_____
_____
_____
_____
_____
_____
_____
_____
_____
_____
_____
_____
_____
_____
_____
_____
_____
_____
_____
_____
_____
_____
_____

"Social engineering has become about 75% of an average hacker's toolkit, and for the most successful hackers, it reaches 90% or more."

– John McAfee

Chapter 12: Social Engineering

The Art Of Human Hacking

There are several social engineering techniques employed to deceive (read manipulate) others. Some can be mild and harmless while others come off as being sinister and requiring you to be careful of your relations with said person.

The truth is, we have all been tricked by a social engineer at one point or the other. It is as simple as a friend using trickery to obtain favors from an unsuspecting you. The aftermath is usually the same – you end up with feelings of sadness or anger, and it may even damage your relationship with the person irreparably. Thus, the question then becomes; how do you protect yourself from social engineering?

The first step begins with being perceptive when someone is trying to con you using social engineering techniques. The only way to be successful at this is, first, to be able to identify what the various methods are.

The index below is by no means complete. However, a grasp of these can place you firmly at a position where you would be able to recognize them when you see these methods happening to you or anyone else. So, let's begin:

1. Piggyback rides:

This technique might be the oldest rule in the playbook. At this point, you'd expect that people would be able to determine when someone is about to apply this trick. Unfortunately, that is hardly the case. People still fall prey to this technique time and again.

The way it works is that a social engineer 'piggybacks' on the license of a legitimate employee of a company to obtain access into a facility he wouldn't, ordinarily, be allowed access. It is often as simple as the social engineer walking behind a person who has access to a building, giving the illusion that they are both walking together, then using that means to enter a secure building.

Another method applied here is for the social engineer to pretend like he already had access to the building earlier. However, some "occurrence" prevented him from coming out with his card. So, for instance, the social engineer could explain to the security guard that he forgot his keys at home or that it was in his car and that he couldn't possibly go back to grab them. In this way, the social engineer preys on the human need to help others.

2. Social media engineering:

Social media is an extraordinary place to connect with friends and family. No doubt, no one can accurately predict the number of friendships and meaningful relationships that have begun or flourished with the aid of social media. It is because of this ease of connectivity that social engineer loves social media.

Sites such as Facebook and Instagram provide the social engineer with all the information he needs about any targeted victim. He no longer needs to go on a search for information about the person's reading habits, friends, hobbies, etc. With social media, he can easily lay his hand on such information and might often manipulate such details to track the person.

The social engineer may use such information to create a relationship with the person, build trust over a length of time, and then strike. Through this means, he gathers more information from the person and then uses such information to cause harm in the future.

Also, he could view the person's pictures to know the daily routine of the person. He would then show up at any of such locations and attempt to social engineer the person in that neutral safe environment. People who do not secure sensitive data such as the date of birth, college, etc. may also fall prey to social engineers because such information can also get used in attacks.

3. Sex can get one anywhere:

This philosophy is one that most social engineers agree with because as far back as anyone can remember, sex has been as successful a weapon as any other (or more successful) in getting people to do what they, typically, would not. Physical/sexual attraction can be a powerful motivating force, and humans may act irrationally should they get the sense that some mutual attraction exists between them and another party.

Social engineers recognize the power of this and would often make the other party feel that they are interested in them. He leads this person on, and this way finds it easy to manipulate the person.

What the social engineer aims to do here is to build a level of trust with this person. When the person trusts the social engineer, they can let down their guards and would not be as careful as they would typically be about handing out information.

This trick will never get old. If humans continue to be sexual beings, there would always be the chance of being manipulated based on physical/sexual attraction.

4. Phishing:

Phishing occurs when a social engineer sends fraudulent emails to a person claiming to be from a legitimate and reputable website. He then tries to convince the individual to input certain sensitive information on the site. The information requested usually are passwords, phone pins, and bank account details. The emails may also contain links directing the person to move from one side to the other. Once he gets directed to the other website, he ends up fooled into delivering confidential information.

The scheme usually works because the site — which is generally a creation of the attacker —

mimics a real one. The familiar environment thus helps to bring down the guards of the individual and therefore makes him more susceptible to attacks.

The social engineer may also do his due diligence. Find out all he can about the person and then inputs such personal details such as the address or name of the person to make the scam look legitimate. The pool of persons for whom this style happens to be minimal, and because of the amount of work put in by the attacker, the number of persons who fall prey to the attacks is also higher.

5. Whaling attacks:

This attack is a phishing scam that is meant explicitly for top-ranking executives. It is usually easy because most executives have their information up on the internet. It is generally relatively easy to have access to information concerning those individuals.

Furthermore, sometimes companies make it mandatory that their members of staff put up information concerning themselves on the company website. In some instances, they even go as far as requesting that these individuals put in such private details as their hobbies, favorite restaurants, and the likes are. It is through these means that the social engineer gets his hands-on information regarding such executives.

For these types of attacks, the social engineer uses the spear-phishing method. He fashions his emails, specifically targeting these individuals using the information gotten off the internet regarding them. This situation often proves to be very useful, and many executives have gotten scammed through this means.

Recently, there has been an unexpected rise in the number of whaling attacks carried out on unsuspecting corporate officers. A lot of personal information is often dumped on the internet by these individuals. There are no adequate safety measures employed to make sure that whatever information put up on the various corporate websites do not fall into the wrong hands.

6. Vishing:

This attack is another kind of phishing scam. However, this is not carried out using emails or the internet but over the phone. One means that it is used to get a robot to dial a series of random numbers. In this way, a person received an automatic call to his phone number from informing that his bank needs some information and to contact another phone number. Subsequently, when he calls the other number, he is then asked to provide details regarding personal information such as a password or pin.

This process of redirecting is usually effective because the person would not be expecting to be scammed considering that he wouldn't be speaking with anyone directly and may not be able to gauge precisely when someone lies to him.

Another way of carrying out this attack is through sending out manual text messages to random numbers. The text would contain information instructing the receiver to click on a link or to call some other telephone number for further instruction. It is when this person calls the other number that he would then end up scammed.

Here, the social engineer banks on luck sometimes that is why he would call or text a lot of numbers waiting for the person that would be gullible enough to fall into his trap. As earlier pointed out, despite all the warnings about these kinds of situations happening, people still fall prey in their droves to scams by individuals through this means.

7. Get them drunk; get them talking:

Apart from sexual attraction, one of the other surest means of getting someone to reveal any information is through getting them drunk. The social engineer understands this and seeks to use it to his advantage.

In applying these tactics, the social engineer seeks out individuals who have a drinking habit – those who frequent bars after work or those who make a habit of going to clubs and the likes over the weekends.

The social engineer first starts with trying to know what bar the person frequents. Again, this is relatively easy in this age of social media as people often release even such information via their social media pages. Alternatively, also the social engineer may trail the person to find out which bar he frequents. For a few times, he would stalk the person, study what drinks are his favorites, how long he spends at the bar, and whether he usually comes alone or in the company of others. Once he knows all this information, he would then strike.

The social engineer may work in concert with the bartender. He could arrive early and give the bartender some money to ensure that he wouldn't serve him alcohol the entire time. Although he would pretend to be ordering alcoholic beverages, the bartender who is in on the scam will make sure that whatever he orders that no alcohol will get added to it.

The social engineer then attempts to strike up a conversation with his prey. He makes sure that he tries to keep him inebriated by ordering drinks for him. Once the social engineer is satisfied that the other person is drunk, he would then go ahead to ask him whatever questions he wants to ask.

In this condition, the other party would have his guards down and may not even realize when he would be giving out sensitive information.

8. Baiting:

This practice is as old as the story of the city of Troy. Baiting is a sort of technique that resembles the Trojan horse. Here what the social engineer does is to leave USB drives with viruses on them at strategic locations. These locations are usually in public places where he would be sure a lot of people frequent and where he would be sure someone would be tempted to pick up and use the item.

Once the infected USB drive or optical disks get inserted into the devices of these individuals, it automatically clones all the information needed by the social engineer and sends it across to him. It may also grant the social engineer access to the individual's device remotely, and the social engineer will thus be able to control the individual's device wherever he tends to be.

This sort of attack can also happen in the random links that are, at random times, found on the internet. The social engineer works with the knowledge that individuals are too enamored by the sight of free items and may not be able to resist the temptation of a free USB device lying around at a random place.

How to Protect Yourself from Social Engineering Attacks

When you own a business, or you have access to the internet, you must be aware that some social engineer can deprive you or your assets.

It is not essential if you are a millionaire or not, or if you have tons of cash stored up somewhere or not. It is because of this reason that you need to be prepared for the attempts when they come. When this happens, you would be better equipped to fend off any attacks by social engineers.

Most of the suggestions listed below are pretty simple and should take nothing more than common sense to figure out – I mean, you need no one to tell you, if you frequent a bar, that you should leave immediately you feel yourself getting drunk – however, some of them require positive steps that you are not easy prey to social engineers.

"A lot of hacking is playing with other people, you know, getting them to do strange things"

— Steve Wozniak

I have attempted to make the steps as easy as possible. However, the bulk of the work rests on you. These suggestions would only work if you allow them to work. Here are the tips:

1. Learn more about social engineering and the ways by which it can happen:

The first step in saving yourself from possible attacks in the future, which can be classified as social engineering is through education. Although there are always new tools used by social engineers, however, when you can know about some of their tactics, you would then be able to predict the means they could come through in the future.

You are supposed to learn as much as you can about how they work, what tactics they use, who their victims most likely are and other such information. If you are the head of an organization or if you have people working for or under, you do make it compulsory that they acquire the most basic knowledge about this phenomenon and how it works. You should do this, especially for the employees who have access to sensitive information regarding your company.

There is hardly a dearth of information in this area. If you search on the internet, you would be able to have access to all the information you need.

It is also a good step you have taken by reading this e-book. If you follow all the information you have gleaned from this book, then you can be sure that you are one step ahead of the social engineer.

2. Be careful of what information you put out:

As already discussed in the preceding pages, social engineers usually find easy prey amongst individuals who put up a lot of information regarding their private lives on social media. Before you put up anything do ask yourself whether it is necessary.

Also, although you must promote your company using social media, make sure that your accounts will not put the company in a vulnerable position. What you should put up concerning your work should be strictly relating to work and should contain no compromising details.

For companies that require employees to put up bios on the company website, you could make sure that all that you put up are strictly work-related. Do not put up personal contacts, personal email addresses, or any other such contact information.

If you drink or frequent clubs, please do not put this up on social media. I doubt if there is any situation where such information would be of help to your firm.

3. Before disclosing any information, make sure that the person on the other end deserves to know:

It means that all the information you give out must be on a need to know basis, especially so for sensitive information such as your passwords or pins.

It is an absolute no-no to release details such as your pin or social security number to a random person on the internet. It doesn't matter if the person affirms to be from your bank or your insurance company. Your bank or a credit card company would hardly ask you to disclose such information to them by phone or on the internet. The reason being is that they realize how dangerous those sorts of situations can be and do also seek to protect their clients themselves.

This situation also applies in face to face conversations. Social engineers recognize that humans often want to render help and assistance to anyone they find to be in an awkward position, and they tend to prey on that. Also, companies put a lot of pressure on their members of staff, telling them of the need to be cheerful and friendly, and helpful to anyone requiring their assistance.

However, it is still possible to maintain a friendly disposition while being on your guard and making sure you do not give out sensitive information regarding the company. For instance, you need to be on the alert. Anything someone starts asking questions that do not fit into the general inquiries.

More so, you should also be on the alert when it appears that the other person is making a lot of pressure on you to release information concerning anything. This reason is particularly so if the information is one that you do not feel inclined to share.

At any of these points, the right thing to do would be to stop and evaluate the conversation you had had up to that point. Then identify anything that seemed out of the ordinary – even the slightest thing should put you on guard – then consider whether to go along with the conversation or to discontinue.

4. Make sure your anti-virus detectors are up to date:

Make sure that all devices are secured and that your anti-virus software is up to date. Also only make sure that the sites you access on the internet are secured. Do not click links if you aren't sure of the source. If you feel suspicious of any offer from any site, do not make the mistake of even clicking to find out if it is genuine.

Also, make sure that you set your spam filters to be high. Every email software makes a provision for spam filters. You can go to the settings and tweak yours, setting it high so it would be able to sift spam messages the very second, they get sent to you

You still must perform regular checks in your spam folder so that you do not miss important emails getting trapped in your spam folder. This situation happens very often, as some genuine messages may be crafted and be mistaken by the AI for spam.

Finally, do not download files you are not aware of the source. If you do not know the person sending you files, then it may be possible that the files ended up corrupted with viruses. Do not even attempt opening or downloading it to be sure if it is corrupt or not.

5. Change weak passwords:

If your password is your birthday – any combination of your birthday whatsoever – then you should change it. Such passwords are weak and can easily end up hacked by even an amateur hacker. Also, make it a habit to change your password randomly. This situation is especially so if you had given it out to someone or when you feel you have ended up compromised in any way. When any of those situations happens, then it might be time to change your password.

Furthermore, you should not reuse your password. If a password has already ended up used for a particular purpose, try to find an alternative password if you need to generate a pin/password for another transaction

Using the same password on multiple occasions is unwise and can be likened to that fellow who put all his eggs into one basket. This problem means that if someone gains access to that one basket, he automatically gains access to all the eggs. Imagine how scary that could be for anybody – that is what you do when you use the same password multiple times.

This kind of situation automatically makes it less stressful for the social engineer to gain access to several areas of your life at the same time. Your Facebook password should not be the same as your email password and should not be the same as that of your account.

There is hardly a shortage of passwords you can use for different occasions. If your concern is that you might forget the passwords, then you could write them down manually in a notebook. That way, you are assured that no hacker would have access to it.

Finally, take care and be careful to avoid falling into social engineering traps.

If something seems too good to be true, it almost always is!

"Social Engineering bypasses all technologies, including firewalls"

—Kevin Mitnick

Dark Psychology Secrets

Notes:

_____
_____
_____
_____
_____
_____
_____
_____
_____
_____
_____
_____
_____
_____
_____
_____
_____
_____
_____
_____
_____
_____
_____
_____
_____
_____
_____
_____

"You'll learn at your expense that in life's long journey you will meet many masks and few true faces."

— *Luigi Pirandello*

Conclusion

In the journey of Dark Psychology, we explored the secrets of the most sordid part of our mind.

We understood how important it is to know ourselves better before projecting our fear and insecurities on others. But, anyway, we are part of a community, and we should learn how to recognize and use if we want, the toolbox of "Dark" people.

One of the most used tools is the mask.

During Halloween, people get crazy for the most popular masks range, from Batman to Joker and **Dalí**.

Halloween is an old Celtic celebration on which people needed masks to shield themselves from evil spirits during All Hallows' Eve.

Still, after thousands of years, people are

wearing masks, hiding behind anything from a false smile to headphones to my personal favourite: people wearing dark glasses in the night—and I'm sure they are not even VIP.

Here we are talking about emotional masks, the masks we hide behind because of fear. For instance, If we are not sure of our power, we can use the mask of a bully. If we think the world doesn't love us, we can wear a mask of anger. We mask the debts that we should pay for a lifestyle we can't afford; we think that everything is okay at work even if we are close to being fired; we want to see that things are okay in our marriages when there is distance.

Luigi Pirandello, a famous Italian writer, in a renowned novel, wrote that we are "One, No One and One Hundred Thousand."

"One" represents the image that every human being has of himself; "No one" is what the protagonist of the story chooses, in the end, to be and one "hundred thousand" clearly portrays the image that others have of us.

We weren't born with these masks. We put them on later, so we can take them off.

Machiavellianism, Narcissism, and psychopathy could be a mask that, in some cases, can become a severe pathology to really take care, with the help of a counsellor.

No one would be a victim of a manipulator, but unfortunately, it happens customarily. Maybe we will not be subject to someone specifically in the Dark Triad, but usually, people face dark psychology tactics daily.

Do you want to be really successful in your relationships, parenting, work, and other vital areas of your life?

So, evaluate yourself to determine your strategy for persuasion and motivation. Doing it in the right way will give you long-term credibility and influence. If you do wrongly, going "Dark," should bring to broken relationships, poor character, and long-term failing because people see through the darkness and realize your intent.

Now, at the end of the book, we would like to do an exercise with you.

Did you notice something else on the cover of the book? Did you learn the lessons from this book?

I will give you another chance.

Come back to the book cover and focus on the title. Did you see now the subliminal message hidden in the title? In boldface, after the title on the right side, you will see: BUY NOW.

This exercise is to experience with you some of our suggestions, showing you how it is frequent and sometimes unexpected to find manipulation in our daily life.

We learned that being aware of ourselves and our surroundings can undoubtedly improve and, in a specific case, save our life.

We hope you enjoy reading Dark Psychology Secrets. Please let us know your thoughts by leaving a short review on Amazon. Thank you.

"It all depends on how we look at things, and not how they are in themselves"

– *Carl Gustav Jung*

Notes:

_____
_____
_____
_____
_____
_____
_____
_____
_____
_____
_____
_____
_____
_____
_____
_____
_____
_____
_____
_____
_____
_____
_____
_____

Dark Psychology Secrets

www.ingramcontent.com/pod-product-compliance
Lightning Source LLC
Chambersburg PA
CBHW070326220526
45467CB00001B/54